"I've read a lot of books on youth ministry, an[...] them, so hear me well: *Relationships Unfilte[...]* [...]tant youth ministry book in a generation. Andrew Root has o[...] tables of 'relational ministry'—and he's reminded us that at the center of relationships is not influence, but Jesus."
—**Tony Jones (http://tonyj.net), author,** *The New Christians: Dispatches from the Emergent Frontier*

"When Andy Root published *Revisiting Relational Youth Ministry,* he began a vitally important and desperately needed conversation among youth academics and seasoned youth ministry veterans about what relational youth ministry should really look like. Now, with the release of *Relationships Unfiltered,* Root has boiled down the essence of the first book, making it more accessible to a wider audience without losing the core of what made it so important. This is a must-read for anyone involved in ministry to adolescents."
—**Rev. James K. Hampton, Ph.D., professor of youth ministry, School of Practical Theology, Asbury Theological Seminary**

"People in our culture who are outside of the church have come to the conclusion that Christians, too often, have an agenda for relationships. Even though adolescents are still learning the complexities of relationships, they can sense when they are someone's project. Through *Relationships Unfiltered* Root fleshes out a vital theological correction for a flawed youth ministry philosophy built on using relational influence and 'earning the right to be heard.' I believe that Andy Root is emerging as one of the most significant theological voices within youth ministry. Several years ago I was confronted at an International Youth Ministry Conference in London with Andy Root's ideas on moving away from a strategy of influence in youth ministry to a biblical relational theology of incarnation. As a youth ministry veteran of more than three decades I was profoundly impacted by Root's challenge to not engage in ministry with adolescents by only focusing on what Jesus did but in the reality that Jesus Christ is present among us right now. Youth ministry is about participating with young people in the living, real presence of God in the everyday world. Youth ministry—in fact, the entire church—would benefit from digging into *Relationships Unfiltered.*"
—**Mike King (www.king.typepad.com), president, Youthfront; author,** *Presence-Centered Youth Ministry: Guiding Students into Spiritual Formation*

"It's so refreshing to find an approach to building relationships with young people that's prepared to let go of the usual hidden agendas, of seeing relationships as means to an end rather than possessing great value in and of themselves. *Relationships Unfiltered* is practically written for teams to read and reflect upon, and it has theological bite."
—**Jonny Baker, UK-based author, blogger, songwriter, and voice in the global conversation about alternative worship, mission, and the emerging church**

"In *Relationships Unfiltered*, Andy Root turns conventional wisdom about 'relational' youth ministry on its ear, challenging the unexamined assumptions that have been at the foundation of youth ministry for the last five to six decades. If we have ears to hear, Andy's message will unsettle us. If you're in search of a youth ministry book that will rehash and reaffirm everything you've always believed about youth ministry, stay away from this book."
—**Mark DeVries, author, *Sustainable Youth Ministry*; veteran youth pastor; founder, Youth Ministry Architects**

"*Relationships Unfiltered* is especially well designed for volunteer leadership teams with thoughtful discussion questions for each chapter. If you only have time to read through one book with your leadership team this year—this is the one!"
—**Dr. Mark W. Cannister, Gordon College**
(reviewed for *YouthWorker Journal*)

"*Relationships Unfiltered* is the single most important youth ministry book in a generation."

Tony Jones, author, *The New Christians*

RELATIONSHIPS
UNFILTERED

HELP FOR YOUTH WORKERS, VOLUNTEERS, AND PARENTS ON CREATING AUTHENTIC RELATIONSHIPS

ANDREW ROOT

 ZONDERVAN®

ZONDERVAN.com/
AUTHORTRACKER
follow your favorite authors

 youth
specialties

YOUTH SPECIALTIES

Relationships Unfiltered: Help for Youth Workers, Volunteers, and Parents on Creating Authentic Relationships
Copyright 2009 by Andrew Root

Youth Specialties resources, 300 S. Pierce St., El Cajon, CA 92020 are published by Zondervan, 5300 Patterson Ave. SE, Grand Rapids, MI 49530.

ISBN 978-0-310-66875-6

Cover design by Toolbox Studios
Interior design by Brandi Etheredge Design

Printed in the United States of America

09 10 11 12 13 14 • 20 19 18 17 16 15 14 13 12 11 10 9 8 7 6 5 4 3 2

To my first YM4572 class Spring 2006, Luther Seminary:
Your passion assured me this thesis needed a broader hearing.
Thank you.

(Jen Amos, Kaia Draijer, Kandi Elliott, Ali Grosskopt,
Amber Hager, Heidi Helling, Audrey Keller, Matt Mass,
Becca Martin, Trent Ostman, Amy Santoriello,
Lisa Wannigma, and my then-TA Jeremy Myers.)

CONTENTS

PREFACE

DULCE DE LECHE CAME INTO MY LIFE DURING A SUMMER of anticipation.

My wife and I were living in Princeton, New Jersey; she was pregnant with our first child, and I was finishing my Ph.D. and cultivating the embryonic ideas that would be part of my first book, *Revisiting Relational Youth Ministry*. One hot Sunday afternoon in August, stir crazy and huge, my wife suggested we take a walk over to Whole Foods Market, just a few blocks from our apartment. She wanted to wander the air-conditioned aisles reading the labels on exotic and organic things and check out the free food samples offered throughout the store. We wandered (and ate) our way through imported pineapple and mango, fancy Italian and German cheeses, and dark Belgian chocolate shavings. Approaching the freezer section, we saw a woman offering ice cream samples. I scooped it into my mouth. It was smooth and ribboned with caramel flavors; my taste buds exploded, and I blurted out loudly, "What is this?" It was dulce de leche, and after stocking up on a few pints (it only came in pints), I gleefully announced to the checkout clerk that I'd found my new favorite dessert.

Some time later, my wife tried making dulce de leche. It involved boiling a can of sweetened condensed milk for several hours. As the slow boiling process unfolded, the liquid reduced, eventually leaving a thick, deep golden-brown syrup that was less than a fifth the volume of the original liquid.

This book in many ways is a "dulce de leche" version of my first book, *Revisiting Relational Youth Ministry: From a Strategy of Influence to a Theology of Incarnation* (IVP 2007). The book you're holding is *not* a watered-down version; it's written for a broader audience, stripped of the footnotes and direct conversation with Bonhoeffer, as well as the philosophical perspective on relationality. Instead, call this book condensed, concentrated. It's sweeter and more palatable—not in the sense of being better, but in the sense of being more direct and more concerned about evoking your thoughts and feelings than making consistent and complex academic arguments.

This book no doubt makes an argument—and one I believe is very theological in nature—but it does so through story, example, and invitation, not through big words or complicated concepts. It's reduced so it might taste better, especially in the mouths of beginning youth workers, volunteers, and parents. My greatest hope is if you're the paid youth pastor or youth director that you'd read *Revisiting Relational Youth Ministry* and then get together volunteers, parents, and others in your congregation to read this book. These two books work together: The other more academic, this one much more practical; the other for the theologically/academically inclined youth worker, this one for all youth workers who're thinking about what they're doing and why.

The theological argument is the same in the two books: Relational youth ministry should avoid being about influencing kids toward some end (whether that means going to church or youth group, praying a prayer of salvation, attending camp, or avoiding immoral behavior) and should instead seek to follow a God manifested in the person of Jesus Christ, who suffers with us by encountering us in relationship. Relational ministry should be about sharing the place of young people as Jesus Christ shares ours, rather than about influencing them.

But in the same way that creating dulce de leche involves reducing liquid over heat for a long period of time, creating this book involved a lengthy, bubbling process as well. Where the mixture for *Revisiting Relational Youth Ministry* was stirred in the libraries and seminar rooms of Princeton Theological Seminary using the rich ingredients of my teachers, mentors, and colleagues, this book has been condensed down and made more palatable to a wider audience by heating and stirring the contents in fellowship halls of local churches and classrooms of colleges and seminaries. The process of condensing this argument has come through conversations and presentations around the county and the world with youth workers, volunteers, and parents. *Revisiting Relational Youth Ministry* was written in the midst of deep intellectual reflection; this book was written in the midst of deep connection to those *doing* ministry.

This book's boiling process began in my second semester on the faculty of Luther Seminary after I decided to teach a class on relational youth ministry. The students in this class were brave enough not only to take a full elective from a new professor but also to continue asking me questions throughout the course; it was through their conversations that the cooking process began. In fact, through observing them grab the ideas, I noticed the ideas changing their understanding of ministry (and themselves); it was then that I recognized the need to condense this work for you. I owe that first YM4572 class at Luther Seminary a great debt of thanks, and therefore it is to them and their ministries that I dedicate this work (see their names on the dedication page).

One of my very talented students was kind enough to spend part of her summer writing the discussion questions found at the end of each chapter. I hope you can use these questions to hash out the ideas in this book with others in your congregation. I would like to thank Amber Espinosa for her diligent work on the discussion questions; her future is a bright one.

I first met Jay Howver in a pub in England, and it is to him that I owe the thanks for claiming this book for *Youth Specialities/ Zondervan* and placing me in such good hands with the YS staff and my developmental editor Dave Urbanski. It has been a pleasure to work with them all.

Finally, my deepest thanks go to my children, Maisy and Owen, and my wife Kara. I thank them so much for the inspiration that finds its way into the pages of this work in story and analogy. But mostly I thank them for their love and patience. Living my life with them reminds me daily that I am a very rich man, blessed with such beautiful children and a wonderful friend and partner. My heart beats for only you.

And now to the God who holds all that is broken and dead and makes life out it, be the glory for ever and ever.

Andrew Root, Ph.D.
Just an Ordinary Tuesday in November

CHAPTER 1

WHAT RELATIONAL YOUTH MINISTRY IS *NOT*[1]

MY JOURNEY

I was sitting across from her at her kitchen table when she said it.

Staring at me with eyes full of passion and a smile that expressed her excitement, she said, "We want you to do relational ministry with these kids; we want you to be incarnational because that's what they need. They need Jesus."

I returned the same intense stare with a nod of enthusiasm; I was ready to be relational and incarnational—I was ready to give these kids Jesus.

We nodded and smiled at each other again, now with less intensity. She, the chair of the youth ministry committee, grabbed my hand and invited the junior high pastor to pray a blessing upon our new endeavor. That was it—the beginning of my stint as outreach minister at a church in Los Angeles.

It may have been a stint—I was only there for two years—but my time there would forever change me and my ideas about youth ministry...specifically, relational ministry. Four months prior to my start, the church confronted what they believed was a serendipitous occurrence. One Wednesday night, for no particular reason, dozens of adolescents began showing up at the church. I'm sure part of the reason for their appearance, if not most of it, was the suitability of the church steps for skateboarding, as well as glimpses of the opposite sex and the faint odor of pizza drifting from the building. While these adolescents from the neighborhood were happy to hang out in front of the church, they were much less willing to participate in anything inside the church.

It was my job to bridge the two worlds, to stand between the world of the church and the world of the neighborhood adolescent. It was my job (as understood by the youth ministry chairperson, the youth ministry staff, and myself) to *influence* these adolescents toward participation in the church and its faith. I didn't blink twice at this expectation. I had just come from working for three years for Young Life in suburban St. Paul, Minnesota, and I understood the power and potential of influencing adolescents through my relationship with them.

My ministry began on a houseboat in the middle of some godforsaken stretch of water in Northern California. (My apologies to those who appreciate a Northern California houseboat trip—I don't!) Most of the participating adolescents came from families of the church. They were white, upper-middle class, and (for the most part) respectful. Yet two of the adolescents on the trip were different: they were non-white, came from economically challenged families, and were (for the most part) disrespectful. I was told that these two, Jeff and Javier, were representative of the adolescents I was to influence.

And so I began. Throughout the next school year I was thrust into a ministry context for which I was vastly unprepared. I kept trying to influence them, and though I succeeded at getting them to come into the church building, I was clearly failing to get them to commit themselves to the importance of the church and (more significantly) the faith.

How could I influence them? I knew how to do classic relational/incarnational youth ministry; I had been trained by Young Life, earned youth ministry degrees, and read all the most important books concerning relational youth work. But it seemed that in this context such perspectives didn't work. Still, I did as I had been taught; I met these adolescents in their own location and initiated conversations with them focused on things they liked.

But when you approach a kid you already know while he's talking with his friends and say, "Hey what's up?" and his response is literally, "Get the f--- away from me!" what do you do? What do you do when an adolescent—who, only a half hour ago, through long looks and shoulder shrugs, expressed how deeply it hurts never to see his father—is now calling you "a rapist" for expressing any care for him? How do you influence a group of teenagers when they return your favor of a burger and a ride by tagging your car windows with rival gang signs of the very territory you'll have to drive back through after dropping them off at home? How do you influence teenagers who refuse your care but nevertheless continue to ask for it with their constant and consistent presence?

The latter may be far more extreme than your experience, but it raises questions for all of us—most directly, *What is the point of our relationships with kids?* And how do we know when these relationships are successful? Faithful? Or simply worthwhile?

Still my experience pushed even more questions to the surface: *How can you be a relational bridge between adolescents and a congregation from whom the adolescents steal money, tag their building, and use their parking lot to sell drugs, exchange sexual favors, and harass elderly members of the church?*

And what do you say to that congregation when their commitment to the neighborhood adolescents has turned from honest desire to all-out fear, frustration, and new assertions that kids must earn the right (by good behavior) to be at the church?

I started to realize that relational youth ministry was much more difficult than I had previously thought or experienced. It appeared that, because of these adolescents' deep suffering, they were unable to be influenced toward the ends I desired for them. Their deep wounds of poverty, abuse, abandonment, and violence kept them from trusting me.

But it wasn't just these adolescents. As I thought back to my ministry in St. Paul, I recalled many kids who seemed beyond the reach of my, or any ministry's, influence. They, too, refused to trust my relational approaches. It appeared that the only difference between them and the adolescents in L.A. was the middle-class decorum that softened the manner in which they avoided me or denied my attempts to influence them toward faith.

I was heartbroken about the deep suffering of the adolescents in L.A. and wanted to help them in any way I could. But because they didn't trust my relational motives, there was nothing I could do.

Then, in the middle of a fight with my wife, it all started to make sense. She was going through a crisis in her own family of origin and dealing with the hurt of the situation, and every time she expressed her feelings, I tried to reframe or fix her problems. I said things like, "Well, what if we thought about it like this?" or "Yeah, but don't think of it like that."

Frustrated, she turned to me and said in exasperation, "Stop! Stop trying to make things better! Relationships aren't about making things work; they're first about being together in the crap of life! It's only when we're together, really together, that things can get any better! Just stop trying to fix things and be with me!"

Hang on a second: If it's true that relationships aren't (first) about making things better, getting them right, or making them work, then what was I doing in my ministry with these neighbor-hood adolescents? What was I doing in relational ministry?

I had to be honest with myself: I was trying to influence them. I was trying to get them to accept, know, trust, believe, or par-ticipate in something, believing it was best for them, believing it would fix them. But my desire to influence them was keeping me from really *being with them*—in a truly relational way.

Suddenly it was clear that the implicit, influence-centered relational/incarnational youth ministry I had learned was more about *my agenda* for these adolescents than it was truly about *them*. As my wife had reminded me, true relationships set their own terms for interaction (rather than being defined by one per-son's agenda).

Of course, my relationship with my wife isn't the same as the relationships I had with the adolescents in my ministry (in terms of level of intimacy and commitment, to name a few differenc-es), but surely there are commonalities. They may be distinctly different tunes, but they are part of the same song. For example, both relationships call for loyalty, commitment, sensitivity, com-passion, and love. If we assume, as incarnational ministry does, that there is an analogy between our relationships with kids and God's relationship with humanity, then surely there is analogy between my relationship with my wife and my relationships with adolescents. But it became clear to me that when I applied to my marriage the same principles of relational influence I was trying to develop with kids, my wife saw my efforts as meaningless or even hurtful.

I had to recognize that sharing in the suffering humanity of these adolescents had been secondary to my desire to influence them toward some other end. It took the deep suffering of these adolescents in Los Angeles to alert me to the fact that, though we might call our youth ministry "relational," it fails to be so if we have another end in mind for our relationship than being with and for each other.

SENSING THE PROBLEM

It was then no surprise to me when I heard some voices in youth ministry making a call for us to move beyond a relational ministry to something they called "post-relational ministry."[2] It sounded interesting; yet the argument, when presented, made no sense to me. They were calling us to concern ourselves with community practices more than relationships. But community itself is a network of relationships, and surely focusing on community practices would not solve the issues I faced with the likes of Jeff and Javier. Besides, my wife would have been even more frustrated with me if I had focused my attention on my own listening skills or dressed up our "date night" but still had been unwilling to really share her situation.

It was also odd that these ministry voices seemed to portray relational ministry as a projection of modernity, thinking that by adding a *post* to *relational* they were freeing it from the scandal of modernity. Yet, as any good postmodern theorist will tell you, the turn from modernity to postmodernity (or whatever you want to call the milieu in which we now find ourselves) is characterized by an acknowledgement of our relational interconnections, whether based in physics, culture and economy, psychology, or theology. Therefore, they couldn't possibly be calling youth ministry to move into truly *post* (i.e., *after*) relational ministry, right? They surely weren't calling us to do ministry without relationships, were they?

Rather, what I believe these voices wished to say—and what my own ministry experience most definitely did say—was that youth ministry needed to rethink what it really believed about relationships.

What I believe is needed is not a *post*-relational ministry but a truly *relational* relational ministry—a relational ministry that is truly *incarnational* by being truly *relational*.

It may be that we owe a great many adolescents (and now adults) an apology. We may have talked about wanting to be in relationship with them, but upon deeper reflection it became clear we were more concerned about influencing them. We cared more about getting them saved, baptized, confirmed, or involved in positive activities than about being truly with them in the deepest joys and sufferings of their lives.

Of course it would be way too simple (and wrong) to say that every adult-adolescent relationship there ever was in youth ministry has been more about influencing adolescents than deeply being with them. We all can probably think of relationships we have had with a few adolescents that have been truly *relational* relationships—that were sincerely about being together in the mess of life. The problem, however, is that when it comes to the history and theology of relational youth ministry (the way we learn about it and seek to practice it), relationships were used for what sociologists call instrumental purposes.

What I mean is we are often taught, and therefore teach others, that relationships are the key to ministry because they are tools. We say that if this tool is used correctly, it can provide us with the leverage we need to influence adolescents in the direction we desire. (And it doesn't sound as bad when we say that what we desire to influence them toward is "a relationship with God.")

But is influence really what relationships are for? Is this really what the incarnation is about? I am certain (from the experience of trying) that my wife would not stand for my viewing our relationship as a tool for me to get what I desire from her. And by extension, I have trouble believing that God sent Jesus because he was the most effective tool to get us to do what God wants.

So how did relational youth ministry become the way we do things? And why does it use the incarnation as a model for how to influence people?

A LITTLE HISTORY

Jim Rayburn, the founder of Young Life, is often credited with the creation of relational youth ministry. Of course, pastors and missionaries for decades, centuries, and maybe even millennia have discussed the importance of relationally entering into the geographical place where one is in ministry. But Rayburn's relationship focus came in the wake of unique cultural changes. Whereas pastors and missionaries previously were either already within or became part of the local context by moving in and sharing in its life, the youth worker of the middle twentieth century could no longer do this.[3]

In the years leading up to Rayburn's ministry, adolescence had become a life stage experienced by all people somewhere between the ages of 13 and 18. This stage of life came with a distinct culture originally created from the fact that teenagers spent most of their meaningful hours of the day no longer with the family working but with their peers learning.

In the halls of the high school, adolescence became a distinct culture in America, with its own clothing, music, food, and activities. Adults were excluded from this culture simply by being older than 18 and no longer in high school. Most parents feared this new distinct youth culture, worrying about its effects on their children. But it was not only the youth culture that pushed parents into fear but also larger cultural realities such as World War II, the Cold War, consumerism, and secularization. America was changing in the wake of modernization, and adolescents were now cut free from their parents to have their own experiences and opinions of these changes.

It was during a seminary internship that Rayburn was pointed toward this strange new culture. His supervising pastor asserted, "I'm not particularly worried about the kids who are in. They're safe, and as far as they're concerned, I don't need your services. To you I entrust the crowd of teenagers who stay away from church. The center of your widespread parish will be the local high school."

After a few failed attempts at starting Bible clubs on the high school campus, Rayburn decided the only way to get kids to participate in his program was by inviting them personally. Approaching adolescents in the hallways, Rayburn would start up a conversation about music, sports, or fashion (the pillars of the distinct youth culture). As he did this, gradually a relationship would form. He knew their names and their likes and dislikes, among other things. After such conversations Rayburn would invite kids to come to his Club meeting, and to his surprise, they would. They not only came but brought their friends as well. Rayburn had put his finger on a brand-new pulse: The world of the American adolescent was constructed around self-chosen relationships, and if Rayburn could himself enter into relationships with adolescents, he could "earn or win the right" to influence them toward participation in his ministry or his faith. In a time when parents, teachers, and church leaders were afraid of the new influences their youth were exposed to on a daily basis, the idea of using relationships to influence adolescents toward positive things instead was a natural fit.

This idea of influence ran so deep in Rayburn and Young Life's early thought that it became an organizational technique to first seek out the most popular kids in a high school. The belief was that by winning their allegiance, adolescents with less popularity would be drawn like a magnet to the place and commitments of the most popular.

The idea was simple (and sociologically brilliant): Youth workers formed relationships to influence popular adolescents to participate in a youth ministry, event, or camp experience and hopefully come to a faith commitment. These popular adolescents (and now new believers) influenced less-popular kids to participate in these same events, and then the youth leader would pick up the relationship and lead those adolescents to faith. Emile Calliet, a Young Life biographer, explains, "Once the leaders that students look up to for orientation have been won over, there is no limit to the Young Life worker's outreach. The most hardened youngsters are drawn in and are sooner or later bound to come face to face with the Christ and his claims on their life."[4]

Rayburn began calling this relationship-centered ministry not only *relational* but *incarnational*. What he meant was that just as God in Jesus left one cosmos and entered another to save it from destruction, so Rayburn (and those after him) entered the foreign world of the high school adolescent to save it for Christ. Yet while calling relational ministry "incarnational" seemed to provide biblical and theological justification for Rayburn's approach, it did not allow the theological perspective to actually set the terms for how ministry was to be done. (In the next chapter we'll seek to allow an incarnational theology to set the terms for how we actually do ministry.)

There were (are) many Young Life staffers who had (have) moved beyond this instrumental influence perspective of relational/incarnational ministry that views relationships as tools. There are a number of folks who have tried to think about the practice more theologically (I'm thinking particularly of Darrell Guder and those who worked with him in the 1970s). Nevertheless, this influence understanding of relational ministry began metastasizing in the bones of youth ministry even beyond the parachurch.

The depth to which "influence" has been wed with relational ministry can be seen in the writings of many youth ministry works, and it's something many of us have (often unknowingly) perpetuated; for instance, we can spot it in books by the profession's more well-known leaders, Jim Burns and Doug Fields. In *The Youth Builder: Today's Resources for Relational Ministry* by Burns and *Your First Two Years in Youth Ministry* by Fields, a relational ministry of influencing adolescents is vividly portrayed.

Burns writes, "Today we realize that long-term influence with lasting results comes from significant relationships and role models."[5] Fields writes, "I'm thrilled that youth ministry has become more professional...but it isn't rocket science—youth ministry is about adults loving students, building relationships with them, and pointing them to Jesus."[6]

Maybe long-term influence does happen through association; advertisers seem to believe this as they plaster the sides of our highways, the fronts of our shopping carts, and the backs of our receipts with ads. But is God ultimately after product loyalty?

And are relationships really that simple and easy? I would imagine they're easy only if they avoid or ignore the deep messiness of our lives. It may be that relationships are more difficult and complicated than O-rings and rocket fuel. Just ask a parent driving his son to drug rehab, a woman packing her bags with a broken wrist while her drunk husband sleeps, or a seven-year-old who waits at the curb for three hours for the once-a-year visit with her absentee father.

Too often youth ministry thinkers have wanted us to see that relationships are more important than programs. And they are. But more important for what? Is the goal getting kids to commit to church, to behave, to have faith? When boiling this down, there is a problem.

Imagine for a second (and just one second) that this is a math class and the following sentences are a word problem.

Relationships are a more effective tool than programs to get youth committed to the church and its faith. Relationships are what grow a ministry.

Now imagine you've been asked to turn this word problem into an equation. What would you have? Maybe something like:

Programs ≠ Influence

Relationships = Influence

Therefore: Relationships + Influence = Growth of the Ministry (as measured by Commitment to the group & Conversion to the faith)

What becomes clear when broken down this way is that the relationship is not the answer, but a pathway to another goal. The goal is the growth of the ministry, seen in the commitment level to the church and the number or depth of conversions to the faith.

But what happens if after two days, two weeks, or two years an adolescent is unable to be influenced? Maybe something stands in her way, such as deep suffering (like the adolescents I knew in Los Angeles). If the goal of the relationship is growth, commitment, and conversion, eventually I am completely justified in abandoning the relationship. I can say to an adolescent through words or actions, "Let's face it, this isn't working. I'm moving on to someone more receptive to my efforts (i.e., easier to influence)." And even if there's conversion and commitment, I can still abandon the relationship because once the student moves on from the youth ministry, I need to move on to other teenagers. (Could this be part of the reason why kids "leave the faith" in droves after graduation?)

Within the latter equation the very humanity of an adolescent, the fullness of her person (her dreams, joys, pains, fears) is not as important as her ability to know, admit, believe, and commit. In the end I really only care about her dreams, joys, pains, and fears so I can use them to help get her to know, admit, believe, and commit.

Maybe this is cynical and harsh; someone may say it is only by getting her to know, admit, believe, and commit that all of her dreams, joys, pains, and fears will find healing or fulfillment. But this answer only works on paper, in math problems—not in real relationships.

Ask my wife. I must learn to make her dreams, joys, pains, and fears my own; I must enter them with her, and she must enter mine. To love her I can have no other agenda for her but to know her through the windows of her dreams, joys, pains, and fears. If I ignore them in order to convince her to be what I want her to be, I have ignored her. I have decided what matters is only her will to decide things and not the beauty and depth of her fragile and yet strong humanity.

Or worse, I could use my knowledge of her dreams, joys, pains, and fears to manipulate her. But then I am not in a relationship with *her*, but with an idealized form of her that we've both agreed she will be. She will then live as a stunted person, ignoring the depth of her existence, snuffing out the flames of her pains and fears, dreams and joys. Or eventually, the embers of her dreams will grow and warm her, thawing her from what I influenced her to be, and she will realize that I never loved *her*, just an idea of who I thought she should be.

Don't we face this same kind of danger with the adolescents in our churches? We must be brave enough to ask ourselves, *Have we convinced them to be who we want them to be? Have we tried so hard to save them or change them that we've ignored the deep dreams, joys, pains, and fears that live within them? Have we somehow told them through our influence-based relationships that there is no room for the messiness of human existence in the Christian faith?*

And how many have awakened after the divorce of their parents, or their first stressful semester in college, to realize that we don't really care about *them*—just about their ability to know, admit, believe, and commit to the faith we've offered them? How many realize, before we do, that a relationship built on influencing another is not a relationship at all, and is therefore unworthy of being a reflection of God's own ministry in the world through Jesus Christ?

DISCUSSION QUESTIONS

What have been your best and worst experiences with youth ministry (for yourself or your children)?

What are the expectations for youth ministry in your context? How do people around you define a "successful" ministry?

Share about a time when someone tried to "fix" you.

Describe what it felt like when you've sensed others using their relationship with you as a "tool" to influence you?

What role do you believe relationships should play in youth ministry today?

Into Your World:
Recall people (or just one person) who've been there for you, paying attention to your dreams, joys, pains, and fears, even in the messiness of life. Write a letter telling them what their relationship has meant to you.

CHAPTER 2

WHY RELATIONAL YOUTH MINISTRY CAN'T BE ABOUT INFLUENCE

It was a beautiful Friday afternoon in October. There was electricity in the air as Jess heaved her backpack upon her small-framed shoulders and made her way across campus. School was finished for the week, and Jess' mind was free to think about friends, the football game, and having fun. Month one of her sophomore year at a Christian liberal-arts college was over, and she was feeling confident. Her grades were up, and she liked her roommates. As she crossed the center of campus, she thought, "This year is way better than last year."

Jess' freshman year was personally turbulent, though no one really would have known it from her steady, upbeat façade. Since eighth grade Jess could recall an uneasy feeling about her parents' marriage. Things seemed to change that ,year. Their once playful flirting had stopped, and in its place was a coldness that was obvious to everyone. Jess worried about what this meant but tried to stay busy with basketball, her friends, and youth group to ignore it.

A few weeks into the fall semester, Jess was sitting in her dorm room reading an article for her literature class when she received a phone call; it was her mom. In the span of their 10-minute conversation, Jess' world was torn in two. Her mom informed her that both she and Jess' father had been having affairs for the last four years, and her father had decided to leave her mother and move in with the other woman. The more Jess found out, the more stomach-turning the details became. A woman she had never met was going to have her father's child, and the man her mother was having an affair with was the assistant coach of her high school basketball team.

Devastated by the news, Jess loaded her car and fled to the state college her best friend from high school attended. After a few hours of tearful conversation, they made their way to a party. Jess started drinking and didn't stop for a number of hours. For the next five weekends, Jess left her Christian college to party at the state college. Yet, by the end of the semester, with her grades slipping, Jess realized this was no way to deal with her problems and stopped her weekend binges. Having stopped her weekend escapes, Jess got her grades up and met some new friends— friends who were outwardly committed to their faith. These new friends would become Jess's roommates sophomore year.

At the beginning of her sophomore year, Jess sat on the bed of her roommate, who herself was living through the divorce of her parents, and relayed the story of her freshman year. She thought it might help her roommate to know she understood how difficult things can get, and that she would be there for her.

As Jess approached the door of her apartment on this October Friday, she was oblivious to what was waiting inside. Walking in, she found all four of her roommates sitting quietly in the living room.

"What's up?" Jess asked, both cheerful and curious.

"We need to talk," one of them shot back.

"What is it?" Jess responded, mind racing to uncover what she could have done.

"We've been talking," another roommate started, "and we

don't think you should room with us anymore."

"Why?" Jess asked, visibly shocked.

"Because you're a bad influence on us, Jess. You partied heavily not too long ago, you don't listen to Christian music, and, personally, you're not helping us grow closer to Jesus. We all have been trying to grow in our faith, and you're bringing us down. We thought that you rooming with us would be good for you, that we would be good witnesses. We thought we could be good Christian influences on you, but you're jeopardizing our faith by being a bad influence on us."

AN ALL-TOO-COMMON TALE

This is a true story. Well, kind of. It is actually the common story of a few of my students laced together into a single narrative. When discussing with my classes the dangers of doing relational youth ministry as influence, stories like these keep spilling from their lips.

When these stories are shared, we all wonder together how these girls (Jess' roommates) learned this perspective of influence. We wondered if somehow they learned it in youth groups like our own, and what theology could engender this influence-centered perspective. We wonder how they could imagine that it was best for their faith to hurt another person and fearfully guard their faith commitments. And then we agree it's time to move relational youth ministry beyond its focus on influence.

In many ways an influence-based understanding of ministry is a vocational hazard for youth workers and volunteers. Often congregations invest in hiring professional, paid youth workers (or recruit volunteers) because they want someone to help them steer their children away from dangers in the culture and direct them toward faith commitments and congregational participation. Often our job performance is judged by our ability to influence teenagers toward the ends that the congregation believes are best for them.

My friend Jeremy told me the story about his first day as the youth director of a Lutheran church in Indiana. As he was unpacking boxes and thumbing through old documents, a woman walked in. She introduced herself and welcomed him to the church. Before he could say "thank you," she launched into her real reason for visiting him. She explained that her son was going to drop out of school, and she hoped Jeremy might talk him out of it. Baffled, but wanting to be helpful, Jeremy hesitantly agreed.

As Jeremy met her son, he realized the absurdity of his task; he didn't know the boy, and the boy didn't know him. They were only now meeting because his mother believed Jeremy, as the youth director, was an expert at influencing adolescents to do the right thing.

Now all this influence bashing isn't to say there is no influencing involved in true relationships, or that youth workers and volunteers are supposed to be wet blankets with no opinions or demands in doing ministry. Influencing no doubt happens in any relationship. My wife and my close friends have influenced me greatly, and parents influence their children more than anyone else.

Yet, what must be seen is that these relationships were not built around the desire to influence the other, but were constructed around the desire to know, love, and be with the other.

A true lover doesn't decide to love another because that person can be easily influenced, and friends don't choose others because they seem easy to boss around. A husband and wife don't decide to have a child because they dream of making her into what they want her to be. No, we fall in love, or make friends, or have children because we desire to be with the other person, not because of what they can be or do for us.

Instead, a side effect of relationships born from a desire to be together is that we're influenced to see ourselves and the world differently. This happens because the relationship is about nothing other than being with and for each other.

So now, more specifically, why can't relational ministry be about influence? If I haven't made the case in the last chapter and a half, let me give you four more reasons:

(1) Relational youth ministry cannot be about influence because it would use relationships as a means to another end.

I've already tried to show why using relationships as means to another end disqualifies relationships from being truly about the other person. When we use relationships to cozy up to another person with the idea that we can get them to believe and do what we want (even if it is "for their own good"), ironically, we destroy the relationship. Instead we make the other person a consumer, and our true loyalty isn't to the other person but the product we're pushing, even if that is our faith.

A vivid example of this point can be seen in one of the final scenes of the movie *The Big Kahuna*. Larry (Kevin Spacey), Phil (Danny DiVito), and Bob (Peter Facinelli) are sales representatives from a lubricant company. They've been dispatched to a conference to land a deal with Mr. Fuller, a.k.a. The Big Kahuna. Believing they've failed to make contact with him, they realize Bob has actually talked exclusively with him—but about religion, not lubricants. Having been invited for further conversation with Mr. Fuller, Bob goes with the encouragement to close the lubricant sale and save their jobs.

Larry and Phil anxiously await Bob's return. Upon his return Bob informs them that he talked with Mr. Fuller, but their conversation didn't come around to lubricants; it was rather about Jesus. Larry is irate, and he and Bob begin to argue back and forth. Larry can't understand why Bob betrayed them and refused to do the business they were there to do. Bob informs him that the conversation went in a different direction. "Toward Jesus?" Larry asks accusatively, "And who moved it in this direction, Bob?" After the fight, Larry leaves the room embarrassed over his outburst.

Bob, feeling justified, takes a deep breath. Phil sullenly, but wisely, asks for Bob's attention: "There is something I want to say to you, and I want you to listen to me because it is very important... You are an honest man, Bob. I believe that somewhere down deep there is something that strives to be honest. The question you have to ask yourself is, 'Has it touched the whole of my life?'"

"What does that mean?" Bob asks.

"That means that you preaching Jesus isn't any different than Larry or someone else preaching lubricants. It doesn't matter if you're selling Jesus, or Buddha, or civil rights, or how to make money in real estate with no money down. That doesn't make you a human being; it makes you a marketing rep.

"If you want to talk to someone honestly as a human being, ask him about his kids, find out what his dreams are. Just to find out. For no other reason.

"Because as soon as you lay your hands on a conversation to stir it, it's not a conversation anymore—it's a pitch. And you're not a human being—you're a marketing rep."

The Big Kahuna hits on an important point. When influence is the objective of our relationships, the relationships become secondary to moving the product. We then are no longer friends, loving adults, or pastors, but sales reps for salvation, trying to influence a generation that has already been oversaturated with sales pitches.

The movie also alerts us to another important point: If we fall into the trap of making relationships about influence, we too are affected, often unwittingly. By becoming marketing reps for God, we lose our humanity. Acting as though we're on a mission from God, we believe our agenda for the other person becomes more important than the mystery of the other person. That person's story of joy and pain becomes only an opportunity for us to leverage control. We're committed to the product, not the fragile and beautiful humanity of the adolescent.

In fear that their own commitments would be corrupted, Jess' roommates became marketing reps, justified in giving up their relationship with Jess because they couldn't secure the sale. They kicked her out to maintain the integrity of the product and lost the chance to be human, vulnerable, and honest themselves.[7]

But what would this actually look like in the context of ministry? How would I know if I'm operating in this manner? To answer this question I interviewed a handful of youth pastors in Southern California. They were all nominated as doing some of the best relational or incarnational ministry. All of these youth pastors are heroes of the faith and passionate individuals wanting to serve God and love kids. But their understanding of their ministry was saturated with language of influence that saw relationships as a means to another end.

A youth pastor named Gary said this:
The goal for me is to impact lives for eternity. I tell kids, "I want to be the one standing in heaven to shake your hand when you come walking through the door." The whole purpose of my relationship with you is to make sure that you

make heaven your home, and that you're there not by the skin of your teeth... This is the goal of relational ministry.

While this is an honorable commitment and something I've heard myself say, it clearly falls into an influence-based understanding of relationships. Gary never mentions any desire to be with and for adolescents for their own sake; rather he wants to be in relationship with them to get them somewhere else (in this case, heaven). Of course salvation is of ultimate importance, but salvation (at least biblically) is not salvation if one is injured, belittled, or minimized en route to being (so called) saved.

I fear that when influence drives our relational ministry, we open up the possibility of such things happening. Are our relationships simply bridges to get young people somewhere (e.g., saved, behaving morally, etc.), or might it be that within our relationships themselves God is present? Is it possible that the relationship alone (because God is present within it) is the objective of ministry and not where the relationship leads? It appears that Gary believes God is found somewhere outside the messy relationships of our lives.[8]

A youth pastor named Randy believes something similar. When discussing the purpose of relational ministry, he says, "What is the point of the relationship if, once you have it, you don't go anywhere with it? If you don't try to influence them?" But as we've seen, in true relationships, the only point is to be together. Once there is another point, the relationship withers under the heat of expectations and obligations.

Which isn't to say there aren't expectations and obligations within relationships. In my family, there is an expectation that I unload the dishwasher, and there is the obligation that I attend my wife's family gatherings. We expect our four-year-old son to go to sleep when we put him to bed and to help put away his clean clothes. But my wife's point in marrying me was not to have someone else unload the dishwasher or avoid attending her family gatherings alone. We didn't have a child in order to plan someone else's sleep schedule or have help with the laundry. The relationship, our mutual life together, grows expectations and obligations for each of us that uphold our relationship and support each other as individuals.

I wonder how often in relational youth ministry we charge right into expectations of and obligations for young people before we take the time to really see their hearts, their struggles, and their joys. Do we have a "point" going into a relationship that dictates the direction of the relationship and overshadows our ability to truly be with and for a young person, learning real needs?

(2) Relational youth ministry cannot be about influence because then the person isn't important; only that person's decision (or will) is.

When my wife and I first met there were few to no sparks. She thought I was crass and too sporty. I thought she was overconfident and too granola. These mutual impressions served us well. We felt no need to make quick or rash decisions. I felt no need to influence her to like me. I wasn't worried she would find someone else, making a decision against me. No decision was needed; we just hung out.

Then over movies, concerts, and late-night conversations I saw into her being. I saw her fears, her desires, her pain, and her joys. I became drawn not to what she could do for me or what I could help her do for herself, but rather I became drawn to *her*, to who she is—period. The more I saw into her, the more complicated and attractive she became. The more we shared together, the more I just wanted to know her, to be with her.

Of course, eventually it came time to make a decision, to choose to cleave my life to hers. But this decision wasn't the objective of our original encounter, nor would I have been able to make that decision had I not glimpsed the fullness of her person.

When we make influence the objective of our relationships in youth ministry, we often place the adolescent's *ability* to make a commitment for the faith above her fragile and beautiful humanity that yearns for relationship. If the sole goal of our relational ministry is to influence teenagers toward a moment of decision, we'll easily ignore how complicated human life can be.

Jess' roommates kicked her to the curb because it appeared she wasn't deciding *enough* for Jesus. She had decided to drink, she had not decided to listen to Christian music, and she (may have) decided not to attend the campus Bible study. They focused only on her decisions, and in so doing ignored the fullness of her person—which was more complicated than the sum of her decisions.

They tied the decisions Jess could or couldn't make to the depth of her person. If her roommates truly wanted to know Jess' person, they wouldn't have done so by focusing solely on her decisions, demanding they resemble their own, but by gently entering her suffering and joys. (They may have found, if they had let go of their expectations of her, that God was already at work in her life without them even knowing it.)

Relationships in ministry are not pathways to quick decisions. Rather, they are invitations to share life (all of life, its good and bad) together. If influence is the objective of our relational ministry, then we have neither the time nor the perspective to invite teenagers to share their whole persons with us, and in so doing experience the fullness of our own persons and see the places where the grace of God has touched our deadness and made us alive.

(3) Relational youth ministry cannot be about influence because the incarnation of Jesus Christ has nothing to do with influence.

I heard it for the first time when I was in high school. We were all sitting in my grandparents' living room on Christmas Eve. My grandma appeared from the back room with a newspaper clipping. "I found this in the paper today, and I think it's just wonderful!" she said.

It was Paul Harvey's story called "The Man and the Birds." I'm sure you've heard it, or at least a derivative of it. In this story a man's family pleads with him to accompany them to church on this cold Christmas-Eve night, but he refuses; he's in a crisis of faith. Sitting in his living room he notices outside the window a group of little birds that appear lost and cold. Fearing that they'll freeze he dons boots and a coat and rushes out to direct them into his barn; but with every altruistic "shoo," the birds fearfully flutter in the other direction. He tries talking soothingly to them, but they don't understand English. After attempting a number of other techniques, he gives up. As he does he thinks, "If only I could become a bird myself, I could lead them into the warm barn." As soon as he finishes the thought, the church bells ring, and he realizes for the first time the significance of Christmas and Jesus' incarnation.

This is a great story; I can see why my grandma likes it so much. The only problem is that it's not about the incarnation.

This bird story's theology of the incarnation assumes Jesus needed to become human because it was the most effective way of influencing us in the direction we should go. The major problem with this perspective is it minimizes the humanity of Jesus, assuming Jesus only had to be human *enough* to convince us (i.e., fool us) into doing what God wanted us to do. At least to me, it cuts out the heart of the incarnation, which is the confession that God in the person of Jesus Christ takes into himself the fullness of human existence. God experiences it all—all the pain, joy, sorrow, loneliness, happiness, abandonment, and fear. To me that is good news! This God is truly Emmanuel, "God with us."

The God of Harvey's story is not the God who bears the fullness of human existence, but a God who finds a savvy strategy of persuasion and exploits it. My heart stirs more within me when contemplating a God who enters and bears than a God who enters to influence.[9]

It's not just that I find this influence-based, incarnational theology uninteresting (though I do), but also it appears to me very similar to the early Christological heresy known as Docetism. To say it simply, the Docetists held to the concepts of Greek philosophy and its belief that matter (the touchable things in the world) was bad. Therefore, they had a very hard time believing Jesus Christ could *really* have been a human being like us and yet still be the fullness of who God is. They said Jesus just *looked like* a human being, making his humanity a kind of illusion—but a good enough illusion to convince us—a kind of super hologram, I guess.

When reading most of youth ministry's limited theological articulations of relational youth ministry in the profession's popular books, it's not hard to sniff a little Docetism. From my read they seem to minimize the humanity of Jesus and the confession that Jesus bears the fullness of broken humanity in his own humanity. Instead they emphasize how Jesus' incarnation is a model of how we can influence youth, how we can use relationships to get kids into the barn.

To them the incarnation is about how God enters a foreign world to convince its inhabitants that they need salvation, meaning that relational ministry is about adults entering the foreign world of youth culture to convince those living there that they need salvation.

But maybe a more honest theological understanding of the incarnation is to assert that God entered our foreign world not to convince or save it but to love it even to the point of death—and therefore this is what it means to be saved: To be taken up into relational love of God. God so loved the world and those in it that God chose to bear its deepest, darkest sufferings so that God might be fully with and for us. In this perspective salvation is not being convinced of a certain perspective, but coming to recognize that we have been deeply loved and so are given the power to live as children of God, children of love. This is salvation! This means relational youth ministry is not about convincing adolescents by influencing them; rather, it is about loving them by being with them in the messiness of their lives. It is about suffering with them.

Now all of this might be making you very uncomfortable; you might be thinking, "I just want to be a volunteer, I'm busy, I don't want to suffer with kids, I don't even know what that means." Before your panic attack keeps you from reading more, wait. I'll explain what I mean—and it may be that this stance is more freeing and humanizing (not only to your kids but to you as well) than expecting that as a volunteer, part-time youth director, or overworked youth pastor that you are to influence kids.

(4) Relational youth ministry cannot be about influence because the koinonia of the Trinity is not about influence.

Ruth was one of our best students. She worked at a church in Collegeville, Pennsylvania, as the director of children's ministry for a number of years and worked toward her degree while in full-time ministry.

Being creative and sharp, Ruth took on the challenge of teaching first and second graders about the doctrine of the Trinity. She explained that the church confesses that God is three in one—Father, Son, and Spirit. These three persons, she explained, exist equally as the mystery of one. God as Father, Son, and Spirit are equally one God, she explained. Alexandra—whom Ruth called "a pint-sized child with a quart-sized mouth"—shouted, "So what you're saying is there is *equability* in God." "Yes," Ruth said with a joyful smile at Alexandra's made-up word, "The three persons of the Trinity show us God's *equability*."

In the last number of years, great theological attention has been given to the Trinity. Most of these theologians have recovered an ancient understanding of the Trinity called *perichoresis* (literally, "to dance around"). Following this ancient theological perspective, these theologians have asserted that the Trinity is *not* made up of three different substances of God (e.g., water being liquid, ice, and steam). Rather, the Trinity is a relational community where Father, Son, and Spirit equally share in the life of the other and therefore form oneness.

What this perspective asserts loudly is that the *koinonia* (just a fancy word for *fellowship*) of the Trinity is not about influencing one another, but is rather about being with one another to such a point that there is total unity and *equability*—um, I mean, *equality*—between Father, Son, and Spirit: They are one.

The Trinity is a picture of the community of the Godhead; it is a picture of each person of the Godhead sharing in the life of the other two. It would be absurd to imagine that the fellowship of the Trinity is based on influence and not on being together in love, mutuality, and differentiation. It would be crazy to imagine the inner life of the Trinity as akin to an episode of *Survivor*, that the Father is trying to influence the Spirit to do x or y, while the Son is trying to convince the Father to do this or that, all using their relationships with each other to get something else done and forming alliances to achieve their own desires over and against the other.

If we are made in the image of God, then maybe human beings—and therefore our ministries—should not ultimately be about influence but about sharing in each other's existences. For God as Father, Son, and Spirit exist as a community of love that indwells (is with the other fully) for the objective of being together.

SO WHY CARE ABOUT RELATIONSHIPS AT ALL?

All this talk about moving past a relational youth ministry of influence is *not* to say we should no longer do relational or incarnational youth ministry. I contend that we should continue to practice relational youth ministry. Relationships (or what some theologians and philosophers call *relationality*) remain an essential theological/biblical motif, and one that holds great significance in our contemporary context.[10]

The Christian tradition makes the claim that God's ministry to creation is relational. God chooses to meet God's creation personally. God chooses to address (speak to) humanity. God chooses to walk with humanity in the cool of God's good creation. God chooses to make us God's covenant partner. God desires for us to be God's people and for God to be our Lord. This is a relational reality!

Our sinfulness is the problem of broken relationships (with God and one another). Theologians since Augustine and Luther have defined sin as broken relationship. They assert that sin is being alone and against; it is the inclination toward self-preservation ("I'm more important than all others") and self-determination ("I'll decide my own destiny—I don't care about anyone else!"). No relationship, whether between us and God or us and another person, is possible unless we loosen our grip on the need for self-preservation and self-determination. It could even be that the great sin of relational ministry goes beyond *self*-preservation and *self*-determination in that it tries to preserve and determine the fate of *another* rather than trusting God with that other person and recognizing we're all on the human journey together.

I constantly experience my sinful inclination toward self-preservation and self-determination with my wife. After a long day of work, I'd like to worry only about myself; I'd like to concern myself only with my preservation (a ball game on TV, dinner, and no diapers or bath time). But my relationship with my wife places a demand on me that I cannot ignore if we are to have a relationship. I have to realize that she too is tired, has changed countless diapers, and has her own work to be done. So while it seems much easier for me to determine my own life and work or rest when and how long I'd like, my existence is not determined only by me. I am not only a professor who gets to read, write, and lecture, but I am also a father and husband. If I am to be in relationship with my wife, son, and daughter, I must be willing to allow their individuality to determine mine. In short, who I am is not determined solely by my will but is created in the context of the multiple relationships in which I invest myself.

Sin pushes us away from relationship and into looking out for ourselves—and causes deep suffering, both implicit and explicit. What defines our human existence is the constant search for belonging—and we all must suffer this search. The other day my wife, son, and I were down in our family room. We'd put our infant daughter to bed for a nap in our bedroom. Just before leaving her we placed the baby monitor on the nightstand. About an hour later I walked by the stairs and heard her bawling. The baby monitor was turned to the wrong station and therefore failed to pick up her communication that she was awake and needed someone to come to her. We quickly ran to the bedroom and picked her up. As my wife and I raced upstairs, our three-year-old followed. While we embraced Maisy and tried to comfort her, Owen climbed on the bed and leaned over us. Looking into Maisy's eyes, he said in a soft, cooing voice, "It's okay Maisy, you just had *hoatis*[11]; it just *hoatis*, Baby Maisy." My wife and I looked at each other and turned to Owen to ask the obvious question, "Owen, what is *hoatis*?" Owen responded matter-of-factly, "*Hoatis* is when you're all alone and crying and no one is there to be with you." We just nodded. *Yeah*, we thought, *that is hoatis*.

Owen, with his three-year-old, made-up word had stumbled onto a profound theological truth. Sin comes from the reality, which we all know—parents, preschoolers, infants, and adolescents alike—of being alone and crying with no one there to be with us. Our sin is the reality that we live with broken belonging, that we have *hoatis*. And too often, struck with *hoatis* and wanting to solve its problem on our own, we do things that hurt others and ourselves—we sin. At its core, relational ministry is about suffering *hoatis* with youth; it's about being with them in the midst of the all-too-common (and tragic) feeling of being alone. It's not about influence but sharing in the suffering of lost belonging that we all (kids and adults) know in our beings.

The incarnation, as we've said, is *not* about influencing humanity, but about being with humanity in the fullest. It's about God being fully with us so that humanity again can belong (be in relationship) with God. But we must remember (and we will unpack this in the chapters to come) that the incarnation led to the crucifixion, revealing that broken belonging (broken relationship) can only be repaired by taking on suffering. Therefore, restored community can only be found by going through suffering.

The danger with a relational youth ministry of influence is that it encourages the avoidance of suffering. Influence has little room to suffer; it is too busy trying to make a case for a position beyond suffering. The person who wants to influence an adolescent is often not as concerned with living with and alongside the adolescent in his or her deep sufferings as he or she is with the adolescent accepting something beyond suffering. The influencer is stepping into God's role of preserving and determining the eternal status of the adolescent, rather than entering into life, and suffering, fully with the young person.

But to ignore the adolescent's suffering, or to minimize it, is to ignore the full humanity of the adolescent and the suffering God who also bears our affliction so that we might be with God.

TEARING DOWN THE STRUCTURE

I not only believe the future of relational ministry is somewhere other than influence, I also believe it is essential that we tear down the old structure of relational ministry and start again.

We recently bought our first house. It was built in 1912, and needless to say, it needed a little work. The first thing it needed was a new kitchen, the old one being desperately small and inefficient. We called in a contractor to talk about taking out a wall here, moving a door there, trying to fix what we had. I was surprised when instead he walked into the room next door and said, "This should be your kitchen," and then over the next weeks turned an empty room into a beautiful, warm, efficient kitchen (leaving our old one to serve as a perfect laundry room).

As the project was happening, I'd voice my amazement at his work. His response was always the same: "It's all about the tools." Of course he was being humble; it wasn't about the tools at all. I could have bought the tools and the kitchen would look nothing like it does now. He was able to envision it in a new way, to see where everything should go, how it would come together, and what it would take to get there.

No, it isn't about the tools; it's about the imagination, the ability to think yourself deeply into a project, to feel yourself become part of the work, to share your very person with it.

I believe the same is true about rebuilding a relational youth ministry somewhere other than on the foundation of influence. I believe it's all about imagination, about thinking and feeling our way deep into who we are and, more importantly, who God is for us. If we are to build a structure that can stand the test of our turbulent lives, we will need to have the imagination to abandon the old model and rebuild relational ministry on a theological footing that's deeper than the frost line, as it penetrates the very heart of God's love for humanity in Jesus Christ, who is eternally for and with us.

DISCUSSION QUESTIONS

Jess' roommates "focused only on her decisions and in so doing ignored the fullness of her person which was more complicated than the sum of her decisions." Share about a time when you felt judged or abandoned like Jess.

What decisions or activities would you or the people in your context most want to see young people making or doing? When might a young person in your context feel abandoned?

Describe a "place where the grace of God has touched your deadness and made you alive."

Which of the four reasons that youth ministry can't be about influence are most convincing to you?

How does the definition of sinfulness in this chapter correspond to your own understanding of sin?

How is the bird story of a God who "enters to influence" different from the description of the incarnation? How does this correspond to your own understanding of salvation?

Into Your World:
As you worship, read your Bible, or listen to music, pay attention to the ways others understand God, sin, and salvation. How do these various understandings and perspectives correspond to your own? Begin to develop your own description of God's work in Jesus Christ. What is the good news? What are some implications for youth ministry?

CHAPTER 3

RELATIONAL MINISTRY AS PLACE-SHARING

Allen was sitting in his office trying to catch up on necessary paperwork when the phone rang. It was Tonya. Tonya was 19 but had continued to participate in Allen's youth ministry even though she was older than rest of the group. But she wasn't just older in years; she was also older in life circumstances: Tonya toted around with her a beautiful 20-month-old daughter.

It took Allen only seconds to realize something wasn't right. "What is it?" he asked, as the bustling noise of Philadelphia's Germantown Avenue poured through his windows with the hypnotic consistency of waves crashing on a beach.

"We need to talk," Tonya responded.

"Okay, I'm listening," Allen volleyed back. "What is it?"

There was no direct response, just sighs, shifting, and a few groans.

"What's wrong, Tonya?" Allen asked, recognizing that Tonya wasn't one to be without words. As she began to talk, the sound of her voice communicated more than her words. Allen could sense deep shame and fear.

After a number of stops and restarts she continued, "Well...I mean...well...you know my boyfriend Ronny..." Allen knew him well; he had come a few times to the youth group and had played basketball a number of times with the group. Allen saw Ronny as a good, but hard-nosed kid, a young man who had both the reputation and the potential to hurt someone. He had a checkered and rough past but seemed to care for Tonya.

Finally Tonya found the courage to speak directly. "Ronny hurt me. No one else knows, and I don't want anyone else to know. I love him."

"What do you mean he hurt you?" Allen returned, not concerned for stipulations of the secret but searching instead for clarity regarding what happened.

Tonya sighed as if communicating that she'd hoped she wouldn't have to share more but continued without hesitation, indicating that she knew more information would be needed. "We were just fooling around, wrestling at his cousin's house, no one else was around and things went too far. And...well, we had sex.

"I asked him to stop, but he just held me down. He held me down so hard it hurt, and he just did it. I've kind of wanted to do it with him, but not then."

"Are you going to report him?" asked Allen. (Tonya was a legal adult; Allen couldn't force her to press charges.)

"No," she explained. "I love him, and I still want to be with him; I'm just scared I might be pregnant or could catch something from him; he wasn't using anything. That's why I'm calling, Allen, I need your help. I have my daughter to think about, too. What should I do to make sure I'm okay?"

Shock, concern, and a little anger rushed through Allen; yet taking a deep breath, he recognized that this young woman on the other end of the phone line was in need of his presence and care, not a lecture. "I'm sure this is incredibility difficult for you, Tonya" Allen responded.

Allen invited Tonya over to his home. He and his wife listened as she shared her fears and heartbreak. They tried to convince her Ronny was not the guy she should be with, but she was undeterred; she loved him and needed Allen's help to make sure she was okay. Allen's wife, who was a social worker, explained the process of testing for STDs and told her where she could go to get it done.

As she prepared to leave, Allen grabbed Tonya's hands. Placing himself nose to nose with her and looking her squarely in her eyes with intense compassion, Allen said, "Tonya, I want you to know I'll be here for you. I want you to know you are NOT alone."

Allen hadn't heard from Tonya for two days when his phone rang again. As Allen answered, Tonya launched right in, "I'm going to get tested, and I'm doing it outside the city. I'm going Thursday."

"Who's going with you?" Allen responded.

"No one. I'm taking the bus by myself," Tonya stated, with a quiver of fear in her voice.

"What time is your appointment?" Allen asked.

"10:30 a.m.," Tonya said.

"I'll drive you," Allen responded with a voice of assurance.

After a few second of silence, Tonya stated with relief and gratitude, "Okay."

The trip up was filled mostly with silence. Allen offered a few pats of care and glances of support. As they entered the clinic, Tonya was greeted by a nurse who gave her paperwork and explained what they would test for and how it would be done. Allen stood silently beside her. As they sat in the waiting room, Tonya would turn to give Allen a look of fear to which Allen would respond with a grimacing smile and a touch upon Tonya's shoulder.

They remained quiet, Tonya jittery with nerves. As the door swung open and the nurse called out, "Ton–ya!" Allen squeezed her hand, and she stood and followed the nurse. As Tonya disappeared past the door, Allen sat praying silently for her.

Thirty minutes later Tonya returned through the same door. Yet now she walked slowly, her face pinched in worry and streaked with tears. Allen rose to meet her, offering his presence to accompany her look of dread. Tonya collapsed into Allen's arms and let out loud, retching sobs. The tension was palpable. Allen stood holding her in the glare of waiting-room stares until she collected herself enough to show him a paper in her hand. She pointed to the middle of the page where it read: "Pregnancy: Negative. HIV: Positive." And then she dropped into a chair holding her face in her hands and shaking. Allen sat next to her, the papers in one hand and his other hand on her back, ignoring the repetitive glances from the receptionist and patients.

They sat a minute longer, and then a nurse called them into a conference room just off the waiting room and closed the door. The nurse reached over and gave Tonya—distraught and leaning on Allen's arm—a folder of information. As the nurse explained what Tonya would need to do next, she slowed her speech as if to emphasize the importance of her statement. Speaking to Tonya, but looking at Allen accusatively, she said, "And make sure, *make sure* the last person you had sex with gets himself checked as well." Allen could only return her accusation with an expression of confusion. *Does she think I'm responsible for passing this on to Tonya?* he wondered.

Allen helped Tonya to his car. They drove the next hour in silence, Tonya curled up in the passenger's seat, watching each car pass them, imagining the lives zipping past were somehow her own life, wishing things were different, and scared about what was next. As they approached Tonya's apartment, Allen broke the silence.

"Tonya, please let me know if I can do anything else for you.

Please know you will be in my prayers, and remember you are not alone in this."

As Tonya turned to shut Allen's car door, she looked him in the eyes and said with a confidence beyond her circumstance, "I know. You've already been with me to hell and back."

As Allen headed home he felt uncomfortable about the assumptions people may have made about his role in Tonya's circumstances. But he was neither ashamed nor regretful for what he chose to do. He felt more than ever that he had done something truly right and faithful, something truly human, by entering fully into Tonya's circumstances.[12]

Approaching the steps to his own house, he met his wife. As she embraced him, knowing what his day had consisted of, Allen stated in surprise to both her and himself, "That was a holy moment." She returned his comment with a look of confusion. "I don't mean it was good. What I mean is that somewhere in the midst of it I really saw Tonya, and I really saw myself, and I'm confident that somewhere in the middle of this mess Jesus was really present to us both, standing alongside us."

PLACE-SHARING INSTEAD OF INFLUENCE

I have made a plea in the last two chapters for us to move past seeing relational youth ministry as influence. I have argued that we have often fallen unknowingly into the trap of influence. In doing so, we have ironically destroyed relationship by making our associations with adolescents dependent on ends outside of our mutual bonds. So what then is the alternative to a relational youth ministry of influence? What I hope is that we can imagine (and develop) a relational youth ministry *not* of influence but of place-sharing. Allow me to define and unpack the significance of a place-sharing relational youth ministry in three points.[13]

(1) A relational youth ministry of place-sharing means standing in for the full person of the adolescent.

In a relational ministry of influence, the objective is to use the relationship to move the adolescent toward something beyond the bond between youth worker and adolescent. But in a relational youth ministry of place-sharing, the point is to stand in for the adolescent, to stand fully in his or her place. Not so that the adolescent no longer needs to take responsibility for his life, but in a manner that joins people in their existence and invites them to share in ours.

This is what my wife meant when she asked me to stop trying to make things better or fix things and just be with her. What she wanted, and what our relationship was dependent upon, was my willingness to share her place: To walk knee deep into the messiness of her life not for the purposes of a quick rescue mission to free her from the muck, but rather to journey with her within the messiness. In her plea for me to stop trying to fix things, she was reminding me that the messiness wasn't peripheral; it wasn't a footnote to who she was. Rather, it was what made my wife who she was. For me to minimize the messiness of her life was to minimize her. And the truth is, the more I lived in her messiness, the more I realized my own, recognizing that somehow we shared (bore) each other's messiness.

Allen stood in for Tonya; he became her place-sharer. Allen had deep opinions; he wanted Tonya to press charges on Ronny or at the very least break up with him. Yet, he trusted that somewhere in the midst of this difficult situation God was present. All along, Allen's greatest desire was to stand in for Tonya, to join her on this heartbreaking journey. He offered advice, resources, and direction, but more than anything else he offered his presence. His presence assured Tonya that she wasn't bearing this situation alone; another was with and for her in the ugliness and shame of this tragic happening.

Dietrich Bonhoeffer was a pastor and theologian arrested for crimes against the Nazi government. In the last days of World War II, he was sentenced to death in a concentration camp in the Bavarian forest. Bonhoeffer was one of a handful of prisoners to be loaded into a truck and sent to their deaths. The drive from Berlin to the concentration camp at Flossenburg was a few days' journey. Along the way Bonhoeffer became close with a fellow prisoner, a Russian solider who spent the hours of the journey teaching Bonhoeffer Russian.

One evening the truck stopped for the night, and the prisoners were locked up together. It became clear that the Allied Forces would make it to Germany too late for many of them. As a number of his fellow prisoners sensed this would be the end for many, Pastor Bonhoeffer was asked to lead them in a service of worship and to administer communion. He agreed, but as they rose to make arrangements for the service, Bonhoeffer's Russian friend refused. As an atheist communist he felt it would be hypocritical for him to partake. Upon his explanation Bonhoeffer sat and stated that then neither would he partake, for in leaving his friend for the communion table, he may in the end be leaving Christ because, for Bonhoeffer, Christ is first found in relationship.

Bonhoeffer held strongly to the position that God in Christ shares our place and we then are called to do the same. He contended that Jesus stood with and for his Russian friend, and in obedience Bonhoeffer was called to do the same. The point was not to get the person to some other end, but to share freely and deeply in each other's presence. It is in this relational presence of place-sharing that Bonhoeffer said we experience Jesus Christ (we'll get into this further later on).

For one school year I worked for a nonprofit organization in Los Angeles County. The organization had received a grant from the local government to do gang prevention education. My job was to go into four public schools a week and do one-on-one counseling with kids who were in gangs, manifesting gang-like behavior (such as tagging their school buildings or threatening teachers), or had family members were in gangs.

The schools' guidance counselors or the principals referred the students to me. As I looked through their files and entered into conversations with them, I learned of the awful circumstances many of them had lived through. I met Philip, who was extremely overweight and failing all his classes. Under his slow, depressed mannerisms was deep anger. His dad left him in East L.A. to search for work when Philip was five, and he hadn't seen his dad since. He now watched as his mother, an undocumented worker, operated an ice cream truck to keep him and his younger brother in a one-bedroom apartment.

I met Crystal, a fifth grader who lived in a one-bedroom apartment with her family and two other families, totaling 12 people. She told me how she slept on the floor of the living room while her little brother slept in the kitchen.

I met Jessy, a seventh grader, who at the age of nine watched his father beat his mother with a wrench in their front yard. With his father incarcerated and his mother severely injured, Jessy spent the next two years in an orphanage before moving in with his older sister and her family.

I met Jordon, a tenth grader who was arrested for prostitution. He told me about being raped when he was seven because his older sister couldn't pay the crack dealer who had come to their house to collect.

And I met Sara, a senior with a violent temper. She told me about her father, who had done jail time for assaulting her mother. Sara said it was common for her father to come to their house drunk, looking to "beat the sh-t out of someone."

As I sat across from these kids, I realized there was nothing I could do. I had no word to awaken them from their perpetual nightmares. I had no power to fix anything. And I surely had no insight to close up the open wounds they lived with. I decided that all I could do for one hour once a week was share in their hurt with them. Each week, over board games and conversation, I assured them they were not alone—I saw their pain and suffering, and they were not alone to bear it.

I became their place-sharer; I had no agenda for our time other than being with them. We simply spent one hour each week talking. Yet, a strange thing happened: The more deeply I shared in their lives, the more I was welcomed to speak into them. I was allowed this privilege because they knew I saw the fullness of their broken humanity and that my ultimate concern was solely to be with them as their friend. And as their friend I was allowed to challenge, correct, and direct them. But this challenging, correcting, and directing was not done with the intent of influence, but as place-sharing. The relationships were not dependent on their abilities to heed my desires or on words detached from an understanding of how difficult their lives were.

Your situation may not be as dramatic and tragic, but I tell these stories only to make the point that all of us yearn from the depth of our humanity for another to share our place, to be with us in both our suffering and our joy. To imagine our ministries as simply being with teenagers in such a manner would be a profound witness not only of their worth, but of a God who values them to such an extent that God in Jesus Christ bears the suffering of broken belonging so all can belong.

(2) A relational youth ministry of place-sharing means "to suffer with."

The reason I was allowed to speak into the lives of these adolescents was because I opened my own humanity to them, making their suffering my own. I never turned away from their suffering but stared it down, inviting them to present it to me *so that I might know and be with them, not outside it but within it.*

As I mentioned in the last chapter, a major problem with a relational youth ministry of influence is that it's distracted from suffering with and for the adolescent. As a matter of fact, it often has to avoid suffering so that the product it presents is pure and persuasive. Or worse, it sometimes uses suffering disingenuously, like the host of a paid advertisement program who speaks of how incomplete his or her life was before finding this product. An influence perspective is dangerously open to using suffering to convince adolescents toward another end. Either way, the relationship is formed somewhere other than in the deep suffering we all experience.

When Allen became Tonya's place-sharer, he chose to enter deeply into her suffering; he shared in her guilt, fear, anger, and shame. He never deceived himself or her that he possessed magic words to make things better. Rather, Allen believed he was called to stand with her in the midst of her deepest suffering, to be present with her in her loneliest moments.

ABOUT A BOY

In the British movie *About a Boy*, Marcus is an eccentric kid who lives with a hippie-ish, depressed, single mother. Soon Marcus meets Will, a bachelor who thinks only of himself, on a picnic with Marcus' mother's friend, Susie. Marcus was along on Will and Susie's date because his mother was feeling "blue." Upon dropping Marcus off at home, they stumble across his mother passed out on the floor, having attempted suicide.

For the next several weeks, Marcus shows up at Will's flat after school. At first Will is reluctant to allow Marcus in; after all, Will is self-centered, and Marcus is a weird kid. But it soon becomes something Will expects: Marcus arrives, they watch *Count Down*, and Marcus leaves. There's no agenda. Marcus likes being with Will, and after a while, Will looks forward to being with Marcus. After several weeks together, Will uncharacteristically breaks the normal rhythm of their time by asking Marcus, "So how is it going at home, then?"

"You mean with my mom?" returns Marcus, trying hard to show it is not obvious what Will is referring to. "She's alright, thanks," Marcus continues, looking away quickly.

"I mean she's..." Will adds tentatively, unwilling to finish his thought. But Marcus knows exactly what he is referring to, finishing Will's sentence, "I know, no, nothing like that."

Sensing Marcus' anxiety about his mother, Will responds, "So that still bothering you, then?"

"Does it bother me?" Marcus adds, trying to appear stoic.

We are then taken into Marcus' thoughts: *Every single day! That's why I come here instead of going home.* Looking away he answers Will's question, "A bit, when I think about it."

Will can only respond by looking away, shaking his head. Then in deep compassion and understanding he says, "F---ing, eh." Marcus and Will share a meaningful look and the scene ends.

We next see Marcus walking home saying again to himself, "I don't know why Will swore like that, but it made me feel better; it made me feel like I wasn't being so pathetic for getting so scared."

Will, now speaking to himself, says, "I wouldn't make the mistake of asking about Fiona [Marcus's mother] again. Marcus was clearly messed up about it and unfortunately I couldn't think of anything to say that could be of the smallest value. Next time he could speak to Susie, a counselor, or anyone capable of more than an obscenity."

Yet, the rest of the movie reveals that Will's words, or word, had great impact on Marcus. It assures Marcus that Will is present with him in his suffering, that Marcus is not alone in it. Will's one-word response may have been crass, but it did affirm to Marcus that Will understood the depth of his suffering and was willing to allow it to impact his own person. Upon hearing Will's utterance, Marcus is assured that Will joins him in his suffering, that he is not alone with his fear, and that Will is his place-sharer.

Now, of course I don't believe that we as youth workers should construct a whole practice of ministry via cursing. That's not the point anyway. Instead I believe an ability to peer deeply into adolescents' lives and a willingness to see their suffering and pain are essential parts of being a place-sharer. Upon seeing it we must be able (and maybe with more words than one) to say, "I can see how you are hurting. That must be difficult. I'm sorry you have to deal with that."[14]

In saying these words we join adolescents in their suffering; we become their place-sharers. We hope and pray for their healing and overcoming of this or that suffering, but we know that suffering is part of the human condition, and we are content to live together with our wounds—some now only scars, some still open and bleeding.

When my son was born, I wanted to write a little lullaby I could sing to him. I was a Ph.D. student at the time he was born, and I was reading and writing a lot about suffering and relationship. I knew he had a life of suffering and pain ahead of him, and that I could do nothing to shield him from it. Yet I also believed (and still do) that life's beauty rests in our ability to be honest about our suffering and to invite others to join us in it. I believed (and still do) that while suffering is painful and difficult, when another meets us in it, it is nothing to fear.

So I decided my lullaby would have to encompass all of these realities (yes, I am weird). So whenever he cried in the middle of the night, or I rocked him to sleep, I would sing, "Owen dear, do not fear. Do not fear; your Daddy is here. You might be sad, you may be scared, BUT you're not alone." That song remains my promise to my son (and now my daughter as well), that although I cannot take away the suffering they will go through, I can and will always stand with them in it. They will never be alone, no matter how dark and deep their suffering becomes in life. This is the same promise given to adolescents in a relational youth ministry of place-sharing.

(3) A relational youth ministry of place-sharing is a richer picture of the incarnation and the koinonia of the Trinity.

Both Dietrich Bonhoeffer and Karl Barth assert that "Jesus Christ is the man who is for others."[15] God in the humanity of Jesus Christ shows that God is for us and is with us. The incarnation reveals that God is a place-sharer, that God in Christ is *the* place-sharer. It shows us that God desires to join us by taking our place and living with and for us.

This place-sharing perspective is also a picture of how the mystery of the Trinity works. Some theologians point out that all three persons of the Trinity point away from themselves by representing (or place-sharing) the others. The work of the Spirit is to witness to Jesus Christ. Jesus states that he does only what the Father tells him to do. And the Father is content to be revealed fully in life of the Son who is made known by the Spirit.

Therefore, within the Trinity is a relational desire to be with and for each other. This desire to be with and for, some theologians tell us, was the motivation for the Trinity to freely choose to create the world. God desired to be with and for another in love, to place-share creation.

AN INTERMISSION

I can imagine that you are having at least one of two reactions so far. You may be thinking, *Okay, I can see what you're doing with a relational youth ministry of influence. I can see how this could be dangerous, but I am not yet convinced of this place-sharing thing.* Or you might be thinking, *Yeah, I see this, but I think I am doing place-sharing, not influence. So I'm already involved in this.*

If the latter is the case, great! My hope has been that those already doing this might more clearly see the difference and can continue to avoid influence by living more deeply into place-sharing. In the next chapters I hope you'll be deepened further in your commitment and theological understanding of a relational youth ministry of place-sharing. I invite you to keep reading with the hope that what follows will sharpen your present practice.

For those not yet convinced, or with lingering questions, I invite you also to keep reading. In the next three chapters, I will articulate more fully how a relational youth ministry of place-sharing is fueled by Christology (our theology of Jesus). I will lay this out by giving concrete direction on how we can do a relational youth ministry of place-sharing. The final two chapters will examine how God is present in relationships of place-sharing and finally, how place-sharing might look in your youth ministry.

DISCUSSION QUESTIONS

When have you had a relationship to the extent that you "shared (bore) each other's messiness" in a relationship of place-sharing?

Root writes, "Yet, a strange thing happened. The more deeply I shared in their lives, the more I was welcomed to speak into it." How is challenging, correcting, and directing (described on p. 55) different from using a relationship as a tool for influence?

Look back at the three points about a relational youth ministry of place-sharing (p. 52-60). Which is the most significant or meaningful for you?

As you consider the idea of relational ministry as place-sharing, what are your reactions? Compare your reaction to the two possibilities described on p. 60.

Into Your World:
In your next conversation with your spouse or someone close to you, instead of focusing on your own thoughts and needs, focus on being a place-sharer. Ask a question or repeat the last words the other person says, inviting him or her to say more so that you can more clearly view the situation from the other person's point of view.

CHAPTER 4

THE PLACE-SHARER AS INCARNATE

We had just finished singing some worship song now forgotten when the leader of our meeting picked up his Bible and turned to the first chapter of the Gospel of John. It was the first of our leader training meetings of the year, and we all scampered to grab a last handful of junk food before he started.

After reading the first chapter of John, he began to teach us the significance of the incarnation as it relates to youth ministry. I secretly began to rank who could be most *incarnational*. My eyes admittedly focused on Justin. He was young, energetic, funny, and kids seemed drawn to him like a magnet. *That guy is incarnational*, I thought. At the bottom of my list was Jan. She was in her early 50s, had four children, no time for TV, and dressed like she was in her 80s. *Being incarnational will be hard for her*, I thought.

Over the course of the year a strange thing happened. Justin remained outgoing, funny, constantly available, and magnetic. But Jan quickly accelerated herself up my (stupid) list and therefore destroyed it. I watched as Jan laughed, cried, prayed, and cared for so many teenagers. She was still older than Justin, less informed about pop culture, less available, and definitely less hip. But she was clearly more *incarnational*; she had a beautifully rich way of sharing who she was with adolescents. And she invited them to share themselves in the fullness of their suffering and joy. Jan bore the story of each adolescent she was privileged to know. Their realities seemed to impact her, to draw her into their situations so fully that she invested in them.

Justin was often too busy talking to listen and too wild to allow for moments of mutual care, understanding, and support. Justin could go into a school and attract kids to an event, but Jan could open her person to adolescents and invite them to be cared for in the love of Christ she represented in her presence.

I began to realize that being incarnational had nothing to do with relational magnetism, as though being incarnational meant you could draw adolescents to yourself like movie stars attract paparazzi. The incarnation was about something different. It was about a God who so loved the world that God entered the world in the humanity of God's Son to be with and for those in the world so they might be with God (and therefore have salvation). To be incarnational in youth ministry has little to do with magnetism, little to do with your ability to attract adolescents with your aura of "cool." But it has everything to do with gently entering the lives of adolescents as we invite them to enter our own. It has everything to do with place-sharing.

WHO VERSUS HOW

In my sophomore year at a Christian college, my religion professor posed a provocative question to the class. He asked us, now a half semester through learning the basics of theology and feeling confident, "Where is Jesus' body buried? If we wanted to visit his grave site, where would we go?" The class paused; no hands shot up. Everyone was silent in deep contemplation. Many of us had just finished taking a semester of classes on the history and geography of the Holy Land. I thought to myself, *It has to be somewhere in Jerusalem, right?*

After a significant silence, the professor shook his head and said, "The Christian faith is the Christian faith because we believe there is no tomb, or at least there is no body in it. We believe Jesus is alive, you idiots!" (Okay, he didn't say the "you idiots" part, but that's how we all felt.)

Bonhoeffer believed that all theology, ministry, and faith begins with the question, "*Who?*" Who are you? Who is this Jesus of Nazareth? Who is this one who heals? Who teaches with authority? Who is this?

In the same way, Bonhoeffer believed that the question, "*How?*" was the question of disobedience. How is God present in Jesus? How is Jesus divine and human? How do I have faith in Jesus? How can I be good? The problem with a *how* question is that even if you get a "right" answer, there's no need to encounter the living person of Jesus Christ.[16]

Bonhoeffer believes "*Who?*" is the better question because it's a question of encounter; it's a question that assumes Jesus Christ is still living and moving in our world, continuing in ministry, and encountering our person with his own person. "*Who?*" is about a relationship with Jesus Christ as living and still active in the world.

The question, "*How?*" on the other hand, is absent from encounter; it doesn't need a living Jesus. It's simply a theoretical question. "*How?*" can be solved on a blackboard and then walked away from. But, "*Who?*" demands change and transformation. Encountering the *who* of Jesus Christ, encountering his living person, makes Jesus Christ not a logo for our religion but a living person who encounters our own person (this is the "relational" in incarnational ministry, *not* a youth worker's magnetic ability to draw adolescents to herself, but the living, moving Christ in the world *who* desires relationship with us).

Too often when we discuss the relevance of the incarnation for youth ministry we discuss it as *how*. "The incarnation is *how* God did ministry, so this is *how* we do youth ministry." "This is *how* Jesus did it, so this is *how* we should do it." Rather than, "We go to *whom* Jesus calls us," or, "We follow the one *who* gave his life for others." There is a great difference, as I hope you can see, in the *who* versus the *how*. For even in these questions, there's stiltedness in the *how* and relational energy in the *who*. Or to put it another way, when relational youth ministry is about *how* it easily slides into influence (How can we get kids to this or that?). Yet, doing relational youth ministry from the *who* of a living Jesus demands that we be place-sharers, for we confess that this Jesus *is* living and *is now* sharing our place.

Or let me put it this way: When we practice relational youth ministry in the *who*, we enter deeply into theology. We search to discover who God is, who God is calling us to be, and to whom we are called to go. When we fall into practicing relational youth ministry in the *how*, we become programmers or service providers, seeking to find the best model, angle, idea, or event that matches some idealized, frozen form of ministry.

In doing relational ministry in the *how*, we can easily ignore or not be aware of the deep suffering of the adolescents around us. We become too busy conforming to a pattern, rather than being led by the living God. Or to put it even more pointedly, when we use the incarnation as a model (a *how*) for youth ministry, our focus is almost always on *how* concerns (e.g., *How* can we get adolescents to participate in our event? *How* can we get them to go to camp? and *How* can we get them to behave or believe?). Instead we should see the incarnation as the living presence of God that empowers us to be with and for adolescents.

The incarnation then is the invitation to join God (let me say that again: To join God!) as God enters the lives of adolescents seeking to discover and support the distinct *who* that they are in their suffering and joy.

The distinction between the *who* and the *how* was the difference I saw between Jan and Justin. Justin knew *how* to be incarnational; he knew *how* to be funny, outgoing, and attractive. Justin knew *how* to get youth to admire him and want to be around him. Justin may have known *how* to do what we've defined as relational ministry, but his knowing *how* had little to do with the incarnation of the living God *who* seeks to come near us in the weakness and brokenness of his own humanity and in so doing shares our place.

It was Jan who understood the *who* of the incarnation. Jan understood that the incarnation means God is with and for us, and God calls us to be with and for adolescents. What Justin couldn't do is exactly what Jan could do—meet an adolescent as a *who*. She was a fragile person *who* was brave enough not to hide herself behind the *how* of techniques and models of relational youth ministry but to walk toward adolescents as she followed the living Christ. She never tried to be anything other than *who* she was, and in so being, never asked adolescents to be anything other than *who* they were. Jan was committed to the notion that somewhere in this meeting of *whos*, the encounter with Jesus Christ—the *Who*—would occur.

Finally, what I mean and what I hope I have shown is that doing relational youth ministry as *how* is to do it as influence and therefore, ironically, without the logic of the incarnation. But to do relational youth ministry in the *who* is to do it as place-sharing. It is to affirm that God has shared our place, that God is near to our humanity, that God in Jesus Christ is near to the adolescent. Allow me to explain this further by examining the following phrase: *The incarnation means that God has taken on human-ity in its fullest, meaning we are free to be human.*[17] Remember this common verse from the Gospel of John: "And the Word became flesh and *dwelt* among us, full of grace and truth..." (John 1:14, RSV, *italics* added). It was actually this text that was unpacked in our leadership meeting in the story at the beginning of this chapter. Yet there was something I didn't hear that day that I since have come to see in this passage.

If you're anything like me, your eyes (and mind) easily skim past the word *dwelt*. We rarely use this word as it is being used here. Few people would say, "I dwell with my parents," and I have never said, "I dwell with my wife." It sounds odd. At least to me, it has a feeling of distance, like it would make more sense in a sentence such as, "The ghost dwelt in our house before it left." *Dwelt* has the feeling of someone hovering above our situation rather than entering into it and bearing it.

But the Greek word here, *skenoo*, actually means something different. Many biblical scholars have said a better translation of this verse might be, "And the Word became flesh and *tented* among us, full of grace and truth..." It's not that God hovered above us, free from our darkest, scariest, and most difficult mo-ments, but rather God chooses to take residence among and next to these moments, making them God's own in the humanity of Jesus.

The incarnation is not a wooden model of *how* ministry should be done; rather it is the radical story of God's history, the radical story of God's love entering so fully into human existence it became God's residence. Now after the incarnation we can be confident the human experience is not only known fully (like knowing the directions to the mall) but known in God's very be-ing (like knowing you love your spouse or child, i.e., a relational kind of knowing).

Tenting among people is dirty business. Many of you know how smelly and (honestly) gross a tent or camp area can get after a few short days. I have memories of adult leaders who went on camping trips and tried somehow to avoid the grime and stench of a six-person tent crammed with eight sweaty junior high boys and their bags of junk food. But of course it was impossible. To tent among is to enter the grime and bear the stench. Tenting among has nothing to do with hovering beyond. Tenting among is living deeply with others.

I fear that when we make the incarnation a model for *how* we do youth ministry, we present a God who hovers above, free from the grime and stench of the adolescent (and our own) existence. I fear that we've lost this radical confession that God in Jesus walks among us as one of us, *who* is for us. I fear that we've made the incarnation a pattern of ministry rather than a confession of a God *who* comes so near to us that our suffering becomes God's own.

What I mean is that when we see the incarnation as only a *how* of ministry, we're too often tempted to present a Jesus who's not human, a Jesus who isn't bloody or broken but pristine and handsome with a white robe and a winking eye just visible behind his perfectly conditioned hair. We want to convince (influence) adolescents that Jesus is important, so we tell them Jesus would be a great athlete or a major celebrity— people in our culture who seem to transcend our normal, frail humanity. Or if we do talk about the bloody and broken body of Jesus, we do so to make a shocking point (e.g., Mel Gibson's *The Passion of the Christ*). We say something like, "See how badly he suffered! Now you should follow him and do what the Bible says!" But this too ignores the wonder of the incarnation, for it makes the incarnation about *oughts* and *shoulds*, like saying, "Kids, see how hard your dad worked on that swing set? Now you'd better have fun on it and appreciate it." Rather, the incarnation is the fullest picture we have of a God who wants solidarity with us so badly that God bears the fullness of human suffering.

We need a relational youth ministry that claims God comes to us, not as a hovering substance, but as our human brother (our place-sharer) who knows fully what it means to be abandoned and neglected. God comes to us in the ordinary, the regular, the average. God tents among us, embracing fully who we are, whether broken or whole, sick or healthy. The incarnation claims God is among us, God is with us, and God is for us. It proclaims we are free—free to be human, free to love one another, and free to love God as God made us, human.

I spent many years of my early Christian life trying to transcend my humanity. I prayed, fasted, meditated, and read, thinking that in so doing I could somehow move past the weakness of my humanity. Yet, a crazy thing happened as I looked deeper into what the incarnation really meant. I discovered that God chose weakness as the fullest, most accurate vehicle to allow us to know God. I realized that God was not calling me to be something other than human, but had promised to meet me in God's own humanity (and already had). I recognized my sinfulness had nothing to do with my humanity but had everything to do with me trying to avoid my humanity or degrading another's humanity. I had thought sin could be avoided by being more spiritual (and as it turns out, less human), but I realized true spirituality meant seeking for God *in my humanity*, and that sin actually was denying my own and others' humanity (because, after all, God had become human). I then felt free to be human and free to love myself, others, and a God who was for me to the point of actually leaving heaven and becoming human. I realized that I could pray, fast, meditate, and read—not to transcend my humanity but to live into it, to live into it as God determined it.

The incarnation makes the claim that it's okay for us to be human, that the objective of the Christian life is to be fully human as determined by the incarnate Christ, Jesus. But do we say this to adolescents? Do we look for volunteers who can be human with adolescents? A theology of the incarnation for youth ministry demands we be human; that is the objective—not to be super pastors, super volunteers, people with all the answers, or people with adolescent-attracting magnets. Rather, the goal is to be human beings who seek to be human with and for others in the power of the God who has become human for us all.

Justin could be incarnational (at least in *how* it is understood in popular youth ministry), but Jan could be human, which is (theologically) what the incarnation is all about. Justin could get adolescents to an event; Jan could help them be authentic human beings. She allowed them to share their stories, dreams, and fears, and in so doing pointed to a God who loved them enough to bear their reality and even now stands with them.

This is why we do incarnational ministry. Not because it's a great strategy, but because we believe God is close to our humanity in God's own humanity. Because we believe God is close to adolescents' humanity, loving them through God's own humanity. This is the grace and truth that's the result of God's tenting among us in John 1:14. It is sure grace, sure gift, and sure wonder that God has chosen to be with us so fully. And in being with us so fully, truth (that which is real and right) now lives among us. Grace and truth are now relational and personal; they are the human Jesus who is the incarnation of God in the world.

Tenting with people is a deeply human act. There's something about living close to the land that reminds us that we are human. Tenting with people inevitably draws us near to them as we live with them. Sitting around the campfire we hear their stories, glimpse their pain, and experience their joy in laughter and silent reflection. Tenting among others is the invitation to join in the lives of others, to mutually open our humanity up to the other so we together might be known, and in our togetherness know the Creator, who (we confess) has become one of us by tenting with us.

DISCUSSION QUESTIONS

What words would the people in your context use to describe the "ideal" youth worker?

In what ways was Jan more incarnational—more of a true place-sharer—than Justin?

Root asserts, alongside Bonhoeffer, that in faith, "Who?" is a better question than "How?" Defend this viewpoint and explain some implications for youth ministry.

"The incarnation means that God has taken on humanity in its fullest, meaning that we are free to be human." How does this fit with your understanding of God's work in Jesus Christ?

In what ways have you tried to transcend your humanity rather than feeling free to be human?

On p. 71, Root writes that the goal of youth ministry "is to be human beings who seek to be human with and for others in the power of God who has become human for us all." How does this compare to the goals for youth ministry in your context?

Into Your World:
Gather a bunch of youth ministry flyers from organizations or from your own context. In what ways do they convey methods to influence young people? What goals do they have in mind for youth ministry?

CHAPTER 5

THE
PLACE-SHARER
AS CRUCIFIED

We would enter the car ravaged, tired both physically and emotionally. We often wouldn't say anything for the first five to 10 minutes of our carpool. We soaked our wounds in silence. The three of us never imaged it'd be easy working with these adolescents from this Los Angeles neighborhood, but we, the paid staff, never thought it would mean *suffering*. We imagined it'd take long hours and creative thinking, but not that it would mean being shaken personally. We knew many of these kids lived in difficult situations, but none of us thought it would be so raw, so painful to glimpse. We knew they were self-protective, but none of us were ready for the offensive strikes they initiated upon us.

As each of us was dropped off, we'd nod at each other in understanding before walking to our homes. No words were needed. Like two-year-olds at day care who stoically hold back their emotions until they see their mothers and then crumble as they throw themselves into their arms, we ended our trip stoic but shaken, only to crumble as we entered our own homes.

I clearly remember laying on my couch, feeling hurt, perplexed, and confused. We were being incarnational, and yet we saw none of the results the youth ministry gurus promised us. Relational ministry was supposed to be fun! The adolescents were supposed to admire us, not insult us. We were supposed to lead them to faith, not be led into the darkest corners of their existence. Not only was this not fun, it was enormously painful. Lying on my couch discussing another difficult Wednesday night, I uttered to my wife, "I think what I'm realizing, something no one ever told me before, is the incarnation is always linked to the crucifixion. I guess to be incarnate is to be crucified."

We've either forgotten this, or were never told this, but at least theologically it is true. It's a misappropriation of the incarnation to discuss it without giving at least some attention to the crucifixion and resurrection. The incarnation has often been cut loose from the crucifixion and resurrection in relational youth ministry because we've seen the incarnation as simply a model of *how* we should do ministry rather than an essential element of *who* God is for us.

Who God is for us in Jesus is more than just incarnate, or to say it better, Jesus being incarnate means more than just him entering into our world. It means Jesus entering into our world to fully suffer the reality of being human.[18] To suffer it so fully that it leads to his abandonment and death. The crucifixion assures us that God did not become incarnate to simply influence us, but to share our place, to be so with and for us that our suffering became God's own suffering. In our ministries, incarnation means suffering. It means entering so deeply into others' existences that their pains, failures, and guilt become our own. Incarnation means crucifixion, meaning relational youth ministry is about suffering place-sharing.

Of course, even when we use the incarnation as a model of *how* we should do ministry, we still discuss the crucifixion. We talk about how Jesus went to the cross to forgive our sins. Yet, when discussing it we rarely embody it. Rather, we treat it as if it's a past event, forever finished. And of course it *is* finished; it's finished like a wedding ceremony is finished. The event is over. But the event itself continually reorients us and redirects our reality. It makes everything different, and therefore it lives on and demands we live into the new reality it's ushered in. Yet too often we treat the crucifixion like a birthday party. We've received some nice gifts, but it's now past and makes no real demand on the way we live into the next year (this is why a friend forgetting your birthday is sad and too bad, but your spouse forgetting your anniversary is awful and criminal).

When using the incarnation as a model of *how* we should do youth ministry, we almost always stop at being incarnate in kids' lives. Because the *how* seems to separate the incarnation from the crucifixion. The irony of course is that without suffering we may still believe we're being incarnational, but without the bravery to enter the deepest pains of adolescents' existences, we have yet to truly know them, and therefore have yet to have relationship with them. The incarnation is the invitation to shared suffering; being incarnational is to live from the cross of Christ; it is to suffer.

"WHY IS IT A GOOD THING THAT JESUS DIED?"

Leave it to a five year old to express the questions adults have but refuse to ask, or are simply too busy to care about. Millie was sitting in the hard wooden pews of our church, her short legs dangling, her mind focusing in on what was being said. This Sunday morning my wife was preparing the children to participate in the worship service, explaining the reasons for each element of the service and how and why we do it like we do. As she was discussing communion, explaining the significance of the bread and the wine, Millie's face became more intense and focused. Finally she could take it no more; her hand shot up and she asked, "Ms. Kara, why is it a *good* thing that Jesus died?" Millie had asked an essential question of our faith: Why *is it* a good thing that Jesus died? We never celebrate the death of anyone else with joy (maybe with appreciation, but not celebration!). Rather, we fear death, we avoid death, and we grieve when death shows itself. It's never a *good thing* when a beloved grandparent dies or someone is killed in car accident or is fatally ill with cancer. So why is this death—the death of the incarnate Jesus on a cross—a *good* thing? What is the point of Jesus' death?

Of course, the cross has something to do with our sinfulness. The Sunday school answer to Millie's question is that it's a good thing Jesus died because we need to be forgiven of our sins. But why then would God need to kill God's own Son to forgive us? At least to five year olds, such a justification of the crucifixion seems harsh, making God seem mean at best and a monster at worst. Why does God need to spill the innocent blood of God's son (no less) to feel obligated to forgive? "Why couldn't God just decide to forgive, like my mommy forgives me and I am supposed to forgive my brother?" asked Millie's older classmate, Martin.

Millie and Martin were on to something. It appears that in places in the Old Testament, God—as God—chooses to forgive those who'd sinned against him. Sometimes this happens when a request is made for forgiveness (e.g., in the Psalms) or in other places by God's unilateral choice (God seemed to forgive without the cross). So why the need for crucifixion?

When talking about the crucifixion with adolescents, it's always tempting to emphasize the torture of the cross. I have sat through "cross night" camp talks in which the speaker sketches in gruesome detail where the nails were placed, how they punctured the skin, and how painful the event was, providing a kind of forensic examination of *how* Jesus died. This *how* is supposed to be so shocking and emotionally stirring that kids are supposed to (and some do) crumble with appreciation and then follow with commitment. But the *how* of blood and guts in the crucifixion misses the essential good news (and for that matter, intrigue) of the cross.

The power of the crucifixion is not in the blood but in the person. The power of the crucifixion is not in *how* it happened or *how* bloody it was; rather the power of the crucifixion rests in *who* is found on the cross. If it is only about the blood and not the person, then logically those who have suffered more bodily injuries and severe deaths than Jesus (and there are many; remember Jesus was only on the cross a short time) could vie for the status of savior, too. But the crucifixion is not a story of gore and torture. It's a story of *who* God is, a story about the depth of this God's love for us and desire to be in relationship with us, to share our place. The power of the crucifixion is in the proclamation that the one *who* is suffering and dying in shame, pain, and isolation is the fullness of God. It's the assertion that the beaten man, dying alone, is the fullness of God, that he bears the fullness of our humanity, entering completely into the horror of death, which is the destiny of us all. The crucifixion is not primarily about blood but about a person, about relationship. The cross is about sharing our place so completely that God takes on suffering and death. This means that the cross *is* about the forgiveness of sins. But as Millie could sense, beating and killing someone else in my stead, so that I might be forgiven, is not good news. What *is* good news is that another wants relationship with me so badly he's willing to enter my suffering and make it his own, to bear my existence of pain, disobedience, and fear. The good news, the amazing news, is this other is Jesus Christ, the fullness of God. And now, through his humanity, which has overcome death, I can live.

But wait! I've claimed that the power of the crucifixion is in the person, not in the blood—but isn't Jesus the Passover lamb?

Isn't blood an essential element of ancient Israelite practice? Wasn't the forgiveness of sins dependent on the spilling of the blood of the sacrifice? True, it was, but the blood itself was not the thing. Rather the blood represented something more fundamental; it pointed to something more significant.

Blood equaled life, and therefore the spilling of blood equaled death. This means, at least to me, that the crucifixion is not ultimately about appeasement through spilled blood, but about overcoming finally and fully the reality of death. Jesus enters fully into death—his blood is spilled, revealing he is really dead, as dead as a sacrificed animal—but through his death comes new life, new life out of death. This is good news and beyond my imagination; God has loved me so fully that God has crossed the abyss of death to embrace me, to place me back in relationship with the God of life. Therefore, our salvation is not in Jesus' blood, but in Jesus overcoming death with life.

As the book of Romans tells us, sin is the reality of death, and death in all its faces (e.g., hatred, violence, abuse, isolation) destroys relationship. Therefore, sin, too, is a relational reality (or more accurately, the opposite of it); sin is the experience of death that ends all community. Because I live in a world of broken relationships, I am always tempted, and at times deceived, to serve death to others through my sin. What is amazing is that God would so love me to bear the fullness of my sin (i.e., sharing fully my place, which is the separation of relationship in death), so that I might be free from fear to love God and be in relationship with my neighbor.

So then why is it a good thing that Jesus died? To finally answer Millie's question directly we must admit that it's not a good thing, but a necessary thing. It can't be good (like ice cream on a hot day or getting your back scratched just right), but it is vital. Jesus' death was truly and fully death; it was the complete separation of Jesus from his father. It is the ending of relationship; it is the death of the most primary of relationships, the relationship between the father and son. This is Moltmann's point in *The Crucified God*—it is out of utter impossibility, the end of relationship, that God brings forth new possibility, new relationship, new community, new humanity. But we will discuss this more fully in the next chapter; for now, death has its victory.

The death of Jesus, then, is not a good thing (i.e., my wife's homemade pumpkin bread), but it is a necessary thing—and in that sense a *good* thing for us—because in going to the cross, Jesus bears our death (the death of the whole world). By this, death is overcome with life, ending sin's power to keep us from loving God and one another. It is in the cross that we see the incarnate one truly is Emmanuel, God with us. It may not be a *good* thing that Jesus had to die, but it is a necessary thing, a thing to be celebrated, a thing in which to place our destiny. Our world is a world of suffering, a world broken and filled with pain. "Only a suffering God can help," as Dietrich Bonhoeffer wrote from his jail cell, aware of the millions headed east for extermination. Only a God who so fully enters into our suffering world can give us hope in it.

Jesus' death is good news to Millie and to all of us because it reveals a God who suffers. It reveals a God *who* is not disgusted by human deformity, disgrace, or disease, but *who* takes all these things upon God's own person. Because of the cross there is never again a suffering that has not penetrated the very heart of God, which God does not know in his own person through the crucified humanity of Jesus Christ.

When relational youth ministry is only about the *how* of the incarnation, about *how* to enter kids' lives to influence them, it ignores the fact that the incarnation is the very entering of God into the world of suffering. The incarnation is an act of utter vulnerability, an act in which God commits himself so fully to us that suffering and death become God's destiny. The incarnation leads to crucifixion; it leads to bearing the other's suffering. To be incarnational is to be a co-sufferer, a place-sharer.

To be incarnational in youth ministry is to enter into the suffering of adolescents; it is to understand yourself as their place-sharer. Relational ministry is not about having the answers or being "cool"; it's rather about gently and sensitively joining adolescents in their suffering. It's not about fixing their suffering, but about being brave enough to see it and live with it. The narrative of the incarnation, crucifixion, and resurrection tells us there can only be transformation by going through suffering, by entering it and taking it on.

Too much of relational youth ministry has been about being incarnate so we can transform kids, without understanding that true transformation can only come out of the suffering of death.[19]

I often tell my students that the key to ministry is not charisma, verbal eloquence, or fists full of ideas. Rather the essence of ministry is the bravery to stare down the suffering of adolescents; to see it, to name it, and then to respectfully enter it, to share in their journeys.

I HEART HUCKABEES

In the philosophically wacky comedy *I Heart Huckabees*, Jason Schwartzman plays Albert, an eccentric activist who visits an existential detective to figure out the meaning of a coincidence and to deal with his anger against Brad (Jude Law), a polished and handsome business rep who Albert believes is trying to take over his environmental advocacy coalition. The existential detective, Bernard (Dustin Hoffman), explains to Albert that all of matter and energy (all of everything) is like a blanket, meaning everything is connected; therefore Albert and Brad, the handsome business rep, are the same. Tommy (Mark Walberg) is also seeing the existential detective, but he has decided, after reading Caterine (a French philosopher), that Bernard is wrong. Everything isn't like the blanket; everything isn't connected—rather everything is chaos, and there is no connection, only pain and nothingness. Albert and Tommy team up in an attempt to solve their existential crises without the help of the detectives, giving their allegiance to Caterine and her dark perspective over the upbeat position of the detective.

In one of the final scenes, Albert is hiding in the bushes outside of Brad's (the handsome business rep) house after Caterine sets it ablaze. Witnessing the house burn down, on top of losing his job and fiancée, Brad has a complete meltdown, overwhelmed with grief. Seeing Brad's suffering, Albert realizes he is connected to Brad, that he and Brad are the same, not because everything is the blanket but because of their mutual suffering. As Brad leaves, hoping to get his job back, Albert stands now between Bernard (the existential detective) and Caterine (the French philosopher). Albert states, "That fire was a b--ch a--thing to do!" "No," responds Caterine, "It liberated you from the Brad." But Albert shoots back, "Or did it bond me to Brad in the insanity of pain until I saw that I am Brad, and he is me?" Turning to both Bernard and Caterine, Albert says, "Come on, you work together don't you?...Isn't there some secret deal where you two work together?" Assured there is not, Albert continues, "Well there should be because that's how it works. [pointing to Caterine] You're too dark [pointing at Bernard]; you're not dark enough." Leaving the scene of the fire, Albert returns to Tommy, the other searcher. Albert unpacks what he has learned, and in the joy of discovery he says, "Well, the inter-connection thing is definitely for real…it is so fantastic." Tommy responds, "It is, but it is also nothing special."

"Right!" continues Albert. "Because it grows from the manure of human trouble."

This very funny, slightly esoteric movie touches on something true about relationships that we often miss in our conversations about relational ministry—that deep human relationships are often built upon, or at the very least share in, the suffering of human existence. Relationships that have any meaning touch the rawest parts of our person, the core of our being. The cross is the reality of God who desires to be with us so deeply that God shares in the fullness of suffering. The objective of relational ministry is to follow the living God who has been crucified and is now present alongside the suffering of adolescents.

BUT WAIT

But wait, you may be thinking, isn't this incredibly morbid? And besides, the last thing I would say about the adolescents I work with is that they suffer. If anything, it would be good for their growth if they experienced suffering a little bit more.

We'd just finished listening to one of my colleagues discuss her experience growing up in a war-torn African nation where she and her family had found themselves on the wrong ideological and religious side of the conflict. She explained that for many decades, relatives and fellow congregation members would disappear, to never return. She described through deep emotion (sometimes sadness and other times anger) the suffering she (and so many others) had experienced. As the meeting wrapped up, with the spirit of the room sullen, the coordinator of the meeting—a young white male who grew up in a Midwestern, middle-class suburb—tried lightening the mood by directing a question toward me dripping with sarcasm: "Andy, would you like to go next week?!" The supposed humor rested in the stark difference between my safe/easy life and my colleague's. I responded with a laugh, getting what he was trying to do. But inside I was furious. By no means has my suffering been anything like my colleague's, and I no doubt have had many privileges because of my background. But to assume I have never tasted suffering, to assume there are not deep questions and open wounds in my being, to assume I have not been failed by those who were to love me, failed others myself, or been overwhelmed by the questions of the mystery of my existence, felt like a minimization of my humanity. It may be that we work with kids who've had every opportunity and advantage in life, but this doesn't mean they have not known suffering, they have not questioned their existence, or they have not felt (or been) betrayed, abandoned, or lost. We all have suffered.

As a matter of fact, love itself is soaked in suffering. I once heard an old man say that he suffered the wonderful opportunity of having four children. When he said this I thought he was referring to sleepless nights, requests for money, and broken windows. It wasn't until holding my newborn son that I realized what he really meant. Holding Owen in the first days after his birth, I was drawn into deep suffering. My love for him broke me. My love was so deep it hurt to hold it within my being; my hope for him was so expansive I feared it would smother me. Holding him, it would take minutes before I could take a full breath. Looking at his little person, my own person was shaken. To be with Owen I had to suffer. To love I had to open my own being to suffering, because in loving him I decided I would wrap my being (my *who*) around his being (his *who*), making my being vulnerably open.

I had similar feelings of suffering when I got married. I often get a good laugh up in front of a group when I say, "Life is tragic; all you have to do is get married to realize how close love and suffering are." After the room stops laughing, I explain the more I got to know Kara, and her me, the more I wanted her to know me, to really know me. I wanted so badly to crawl up into her skin and for her to crawl into mine, for her to know me as I knew myself; but of course this was impossible. I had to suffer the fact that I loved someone as much as I possibly could, and yet my heart yearned for more. I wanted to love her more, be closer to her, and to be known by her more fully. The yearning of love causes suffering; it is so beautiful it hurts to bear!

I've never felt that same intense suffering love for an adolescent I have worked with as I have felt for my son, wife, or now my daughter. But I have worked with a number of kids with whom I have had to suffer. I have had a number of moments of seeing their inner persons, of witnessing the mystery of their humanity, and of understanding their brokenness. My love for them has broken me; the joy of knowing them has stung. Suffering them, I am called alongside them to see them not for what they come to know, believe, or accept, but to be with them, to love them, and to suffer with them as they confront the mystery of living in a world of pain, abandonment, and danger. Relational youth ministry is about suffering love; it's about sharing the place of adolescents so deeply that we suffer with and for them. It means joining them in their questions, disappointments, fears, and abuses, but it also means sharing their places so fully we suffer the wonderful opportunity of loving them (of being with them) in the rawness and wonder of existence.

When I was in high school, my friend and I took out his Suzuki Samurai jeep after a heavy Minnesota snowstorm. The whole city had been shut down for days; it was an epic storm, even for this part of the country. They'd finally cleared the streets when our boredom got to be too much for us. The wind was still ferociously blowing, creating three- to four-foot snowdrifts on the freshly plowed streets. We decided around dark that it would be fun to take his jeep and race it through these large drifts. After crashing through a half dozen drifts of soft, light snow, our exuberance got the best of us. Rounding a corner we saw a huge five-foot drift that taunted us to come and destroy it with our little plastic-and-metal jeep. My friend accelerated, we hit the drift, and snow flew like the others, but then we heard and felt something we had not with the smaller drifts. It was the sound and feeling of hitting something solid. This something solid took our light little jeep and forcefully flipped it to the ground. This snowdrift had been covering another drift, now hard and icy. We found ourselves in our jeep lying in the middle of the street on our side. I was in the passenger seat, hanging by my seat belt. Besides the stupidity of our entertainment, something else sticks with me from that day. As I was dangling from the passenger seat in the silence of an abandoned street, I watched a car turn onto our road. Seeing us from three blocks away, the car put on the breaks, paused, and reversed. I was angry at the time: Here we were, clearly in need (maybe even hurt, for all the driver knew), and this person turned around to avoid us. Yet, if I'm honest, I have to admit I have done the same thing many times. I have avoided topics or issues I feared would lead me into the suffering of others. I have often been too afraid to share another's place for fear I'd be inadequate or uncomfortable with their suffering.

The truth is we often avoid suffering, throwing things in reverse to head in the other direction, because we fear that in encountering another person's suffering, we will be overwhelmed, that their suffering will strangle our own weak (suffering) humanity.

In one of JD's weird fantasies in the TV show *Scrubs*, he imagines how infection is passed in the hospital, showing a montage of an infected person with a glowing green hand touching others who then contract glowing green hands who then pass along the glowing green infection to another and then another. This is often how we believe suffering operates. We implicitly assume it's passed on like an infection, like the green hand. In other words: *Don't have the depressed kid come on the trip or she'll infect the group with her suffering. Don't ask him about the divorce of his parents because what then would I say? Don't put two and two together that your most committed leader may be the victim of abuse because that may remind you of your own past.*

Too often relational youth ministry avoids suffering, and therefore lacks the boldness and bravery to enter into the full humanity of adolescents. But suffering doesn't work like the glowing green hand of infection. When suffering is shared, often its power to strangle is broken. Things may remain painful and difficult, but when we're no longer alone, suffering feels (and is) no longer life-threatening. The power of suffering to determine our destiny is broken when suffering is shared in relationship.

I experienced the truth of this on a faculty retreat. One of my colleagues was invited to preach to the 35 other faculty members present. She'd had a very difficult prior year. In the middle of her sermon, the struggle of her year became too much, and she broke out in tears, something not done, and unfortunately not appreciated, in academic theological faculties. As her emotions spilled forth, I noticed my own body language. I found myself immediately turning my shoulder as if to deflect her emotion, and then putting my head down, staring at the table, as if to hide from her feelings. Recognizing my own avoidance, I lifted my head and looked at my colleagues. Almost everyone was looking down, revealing in their body language that they too were trying to shield themselves. Believing everything I've written so far, I forced myself to look at her, to enter into her pain rather than fear it—not stopping, turning around, and going in the other direction, but choosing to be near to her. I knew my colleagues and I were avoiding her emotions because we feared that in getting too close to her suffering we may ourselves be strangled by her and our own suffering. But in forcing myself to look at her, something strange and beautiful happened. Her suffering didn't threaten me but simply (and yet profoundly) revealed her person to me. I saw her as she was and found myself connected to her. Witnessing her suffering, I wasn't infected with a green hand but bound to her in relationship through her suffering.

And this is utterly the call of a relational youth ministry of place-sharing. It is the call to see and be near, to share in the suffering, aware that it won't destroy you, for you have been claimed by the One who has overcome all suffering by suffering the cross.

But something else must be discussed before concluding this chapter. I began with a story from my own ministry experience about not only suffering with adolescents but also suffering from them. I wonder if one of the reasons youth ministry has had little to say about at-risk adolescents and children living in difficult contexts is because we have yet to understand that a major element of our vocation is to suffer. Place-sharing is about more than suffering with adolescents; it also includes suffering from adolescents. This doesn't mean we're called to be wet blankets or punching bags unwilling to confront teenagers (we will discuss this in a following chapter). But it does mean we're willing to stand with adolescents even when they test our commitment with words and acts that sting.

I'm sure that many of you have heard this youth ministry urban legend: At a leadership meeting the paid, professional youth worker was encouraging her volunteer leaders to take the initiative and contact and meet with one kid this week. A little reluctant, but willing, the leaders accepted the challenge. The next week all returned to the meeting upbeat, filled with stories of successful encounters. As the meeting began the lead youth worker asked each leader to talk about the kids they contacted and what happened. The first volunteer shared that he met with Sam, a fun-loving junior who was outgoing, talkative, interesting, and came from a family where it was expected he'd handle himself with maturity in the presence of adults. After the first report a murmur spread through the group, and the spirit of excitement was sucked from the room and replaced by a feeling of embarrassed uneasiness as the group one by one admitted they, too, had met with Sam. Each leader had picked the one kid who was the most fun and easiest to be with. You could hardly blame them; given the choice I'd rather spend time with a Sam than an Adam, the six-foot tall eighth grader who often welcomed my presence on his school campus with a punch in the arm, repeated grunts to my questions, and a departing insult about my clothes or hair. If my goal was influence, it would be much smarter to spend my limited resources on the Sams of the world than on the Adams. Sams not only seem to be influenced by my presence, but they also make me feel good about what I am doing.

Spending time with Adams, on the other hand, is always an invitation to suffering. Placing-sharing with Adams is painful; Adams have learned it's easier to hurt others before they hurt you. And if my goal is to influence Adams, I'm in for a long, painful journey (one that any smart person would abandon before too long), and I'll more than likely abandon him before I'm given the privilege of suffering him, of seeing his beautifully broken humanity. And if I'm unwilling to suffer Adam then I'm unable to suffer *with* him. If I'd not been willing to suffer Adam's actions and attitudes as I did, I wouldn't have had the opportunity to listen late one Wednesday night on the steps of our church building as with odd lucidness he articulated the pain he carried over being abandoned by his father. Without suffering *from* Adam, I would have missed an ocean of pain under the crust of anger, rigidness, and aggression. But seeing Adam as a suffering child whose suffering has been taken up and shared (i.e., borne) by God, I can be with and for Adam as Christ is with and for me. I can bear the suffering he inflicted on me, knowing that in bearing (and confronting) it, I'm sharing his place.

DISCUSSION QUESTIONS

In what ways have you suffered when you reached out to be with young people?

What are your reactions to the explanation of God's work in Christ offered on pages 78 through 82?

When have you loved someone with "suffering love"?

"When suffering is shared, often its power to strangle is broken..." (p. 88) Share about a time when you've found this to be true.

Into Your World:

If you want a better handle on the ways the young people in your context are suffering, then try these ideas: Watch the news. Listen to the young people in your context. Talk to a teacher or administrator in a local school. Visit with a local police officer or an emergency room nurse.

CHAPTER 6

THE PLACE-SHARER AS RESURRECTED

It felt like I'd been dropped into the scene of a movie: Strangers and familiar faces huddled under a canopy in their best dark outfits awaiting the pastor as he made his way from his car to the gravesite, the wind whistling gently through the Maryland oaks. Approaching the casket of my wife's grandmother, he offered a prayer, said a few lines of a liturgy, and then asked if anyone had something to say before they lowered the casket into the ground.

I suppose he imagined that one of her children or an old friend would say one last word about what she meant and how sorely she'd be missed. But instead the intense drama changed into a dark comedy, as one of her grandchildren took up the pastor's invitation. Walking to the front, knifing her way between sullen-faced witnesses in black skirts and dark sport coats, intensity washed over her face with every step. She reached the casket and grabbed the microphone, turning quickly, and—with eyes as big as tennis balls, communicating both sadness and aggression— she paused. As she stared back at us all, I cringed as if preparing to get a shot by a big needle. Clearing her throat she launched in.

For the next 10 minutes, she rambled on and on, pleading with the crowd that they don't have to die, that if they just trust and accept Jesus they will never die, that God desires abundant life for us, and if we accept God's message our lives can be transformed, NOW! While she was talking my eyes kept moving back and forth between the casket of her beloved grandmother and her hand-waving, tear-streaming rant, feeling utter inconsistency between what was being said and what the rest of us were experiencing. She kept saying (louder and louder) that transformation was possible, that we could be transformed in such a direct manner that we could even avoid death and tragedy (suffering).

I suppose the stark inconsistency of her words said next to the casket of a loved one could be justified because of the kind of death her grandmother experienced—passing away finely in her 80s, surrounded by children, grandchildren, and handful of great-grandchildren. But as the sermonette violently rattled around in my head, I wondered about Taylor's friend, a young mother I'd briefly met, who we were told just days after our encounter had washed up on the shores of Lake Superior. Her depression had finally persuaded her that the dark pit she experienced was all there was and that stepping off a high bridge would end her misery. I thought of her last moments and her plea for transformation. I thought of her years of battling depression, pleading with God or anyone to transform her heavy feelings into something lighter. I thought of her little daughter, who was living on popsicles after getting her tonsils removed. Now this little girl was forever removed from her mother.

The spiritual transformation proclaimed at the funeral seemed to exist in only another (delusional) universe compared to what so many of us experience. I know it is true for me; I have spent nights pleading with God that God might change me, that God might change my circumstances, only to be confronted with a sea of impossibility.

After our experience at the gravesite, my wife had the opportunity to sit down with her fellow grandchild, seeking to understand the reasons for her graveside evangelistic crusade. She explained with great emotion and some heartbreak that she didn't think death was necessary. Filled with both conviction and confusion, she wondered why we had to die at all. If Jesus has overcome death with life in the resurrection, then why (if we truly believe, she added) must we die? "Look at all the miracles Jesus did; look at how he resurrected people. I believe that. I believe that death has been overcome forever." Shocked by the incongruence between her commitments and reality, all my wife could do was change the subject.

I have argued throughout this book that we should move past seeing relational ministry as influence and instead see it as place-sharing. I have sought to show that seeing it as place-sharing is much more faithful to our theological commitments of incarnation and crucifixion. But what does this all have to do with resurrection? In the last chapter we placed suffering at the center of our attention, but suffering is not the whole picture, is it? How does a relational ministry of place-sharing live faithfully into our narrative of resurrection? How is Jesus our place-sharer by being resurrected?

Getting some distance from my experience at the gravesite of my wife's grandmother, I could understand why my wife's fellow grandchild wanted so badly for resurrection to mean that death, suffering, and sin were no more and need not affect us. I, too, want that! I could also understand how she could see this as a biblical theme—after all, it is. Yet, what she didn't understand about this biblical theme is that the resurrection is an anticipated reality; or to say it with less theological-ese, it's something that has not happened yet for us. The resurrection no doubt has happened for Jesus. He has overcome death; it has no say on him. His body is a resurrected body, free from all danger, disease, or accident. But our bodies are not. We still die, we still get sick, and we are still captives to sin and death. This means for us that resurrection is a future event. And just as Jesus has presently overcome death with life, by placing our life in his life, one day we too will be resurrected; we too will be free from sin and death. What the graveside sermonette did was confuse the future with the now. The resurrection is now for Jesus, but is future for us.

When I was in seminary, living in a one-bedroom apartment in Los Angeles, the guy who lived above me was a talented musician and songwriter. He played at all of the city's most famous clubs—The Troubadour and the Whiskey a Go-Go, to name a couple. Many nights I'd drive into Hollywood, parking on some back street off Sunset Boulevard to watch him and his band play. I still vividly remember sitting in the dark corner of a Hollywood club, sipping a drink, and listening to him play the slow acoustic song "Lazarus." The chorus repeats over and over the phrase, "Now you've gone and done it, now you've gone and done it good, Lazarus must die again…"

Perhaps it was something about being in Hollywood among people so desperately seeking to get their song or band heard by the right people so they might find themselves transformed from nobodies into celebrity somebodies and therefore find their lives resurrected from the dead-end of waiting tables to being waited upon. But my friend was right, and his song said it so powerfully: Although he was resurrected by Jesus, Lazarus had to die again someday. He was surely resurrected from death to life, only (sometime later) to slide back from life to death. The resurrection so badly sought by celebrity wannabes or graveside-crusading-evangelist grandchildren seemed to ignore the Lazarus factor. They seemed to overlook the difference between Lazarus' resurrection and Jesus' resurrection. It's not that they're unrelated—quite the contrary. But Lazarus' resurrection was a witness (i.e., a sign, a billboard) of something fully true only in Jesus. The resurrection of Lazarus was only a sign of the future, a promise of a future reality. It is true, Lazarus was again standing and breathing—a miracle. But Lazarus' resurrection was only a sign of what would be in the future; for now, he and his sisters celebrated his temporary resurrection while preparing for another death and the promise of a resurrection over which death has no power.

Confusing the now for the future has often deceived us into making relational youth ministry about influence. We assume there's some perfect reality available to us now, free from all danger and suffering. And we assume that if we can get kids to act rightly, they can live in this blissful state. If we can get them to believe correctly, they can be ushered out of a world of suffering, tragedy, and death and into a perfected place. Wrongly believing the resurrection reality is completely here and now has led us to seek relationships with kids as a bridge to an unseen world rather than seeking relationships with kids to be near to their humanity in this world—a world of danger, death, and suffering.

The problem with confusing the *now* with the *not yet* is that it tricks us into believing it's our job to get teenagers into this perfect world. This opens us up to some potential problems. First, if we truly believe we live in another world and that it's our job to help kids "join us" in this other world, we can be deceived into believing we're somehow more holy or advanced than the adolescents with whom we seek relationships. We can be deceived into basing our relationships upon a spirit of superiority, not recognizing our shared solidarity as suffering humanity.

But if we recognize that the resurrection is "not yet," that it remains in the future, then all of us—sinner and saint, adult and child, broken and whole—are simply equal pilgrims awaiting the fullness of what has dawned in Jesus, the culmination of God's future.

The second problem makes it our problem: If we believe that the resurrection is fully now, we can be deceived into imagining it's our job as youth leaders to usher teenagers into this other world. We can imagine a top-notch leader directing adolescents from one world into the next. Of course many of us feel unqualified for this, being that if we're honest, we live more in the now of tragedy, death, and sin than in some perfect world. But if we recognize that resurrection is a picture of God's future and not a complete reality now, we're freed from believing it's our job to be a bridge to the next world. We're free to live faithfully with and for teenagers in this world. To be a faithful place-sharer in the reality of resurrection is to *not* confuse the *now* with the *will be*. Relational ministry in the shape of the resurrected Christ is to live and love in the now.

But the resurrection calls us to even more: It's not only that we live in the now (and do so faithfully by acknowledging the tragedy of the now), but also we're called (commanded) to HOPE and yearn for the future of God. If the resurrection is a future reality where suffering and death give way to peace, complete joy, and love, then the resurrection of Christ moves us to hope and yearn for what is yet to fully be. The resurrection is no doubt smelled and tasted now, for instance in worship, prayer, communion, or as I will assert later, relationships. But this is only a foretaste; it is a true experience of God's future now, in this time, but it's not the culmination or the totality of what will be.

As believers we don't live in another world, somewhere other than in the now of suffering, disappointment, and threat.[20] As people who trust in the resurrection of Jesus, we are people who live in *this world*, but we do so nevertheless with hope. We're not different from non-Christians because we have special powers that free us from the suffering and disappointment in the world. No, what makes us different from those in the world who do not know the resurrected Christ is that we live fully in a fallen world of death and loss *and nevertheless hope in God's promises* won and witnessed in the resurrection of Jesus Christ.

And what are these promises? Ultimately the promises are that though we're threatened by death, loss, and tragedy, these threats can no longer determine our destiny. Rather, the resurrection reveals that our destiny—the final place of our beings—is determined by God in Jesus Christ. The resurrection reveals that only God has the power to determine our destiny. And in overcoming death with life in the resurrection, God reveals that our destiny is to be with God, who has loved us so greatly that God has shared our place. God crossed the boundary between life and death to break death's hold on us so our relationship with God could never be broken by anything in this world or the next. The resurrection is the culmination—the ultimate fulfillment of place-sharing.

As youth leaders we're called to proclaim this resurrection to teenagers, but we can only do this by facing adolescents' world, seeing it as it is, and in honestly seeing it, whispering or shouting through the tears and pains of place-sharing, "Nevertheless, the tomb is empty!"

God's future, which promises wholeness and freedom, may not be here yet, but one day there will be no more death, isolation, or fear. As people who believe this, we're called to take the radical step to live for this future. Though it is not yet, through the work of the Spirit, we seek to set our lives toward a future that is not yet here. This means that in a real way, Christianity should be seen as absurd to people in the world. Not because we seek to avoid this world in delusional positivity, but because living fully in this world we choose to mold our lives not after the structures and patterns of this world, but after a world that is coming, a world we are awaiting. A place-sharer invites youth to live lives directed toward an unseen future, to take on the absurd marks of the disciple who loves this world by hoping for the next.

The disciples of the One resurrected are the oddest of people; we live honestly in the now but yearn for a future so greatly that we take on its future characteristics. In a world of competition, power, and hatred, we live into the future by taking on the future's characteristics of being last, weak, and loving. In this way we provide a world that knows only certainty, immediacy, and domination with a vision of the future encompassed in the faith, hope, and love made possible by the resurrection of Jesus, who has been crucified as our place-sharer.

All this means that a relational ministry of place-sharing is a ministry that lives honestly in the now of suffering but in so doing hopes in God's promises. The objective of relational ministry is not to make kids know rightly or be right but to hope with them by being with them. Our job is to hope with them as we suffer with them. In this way we together become people of the resurrection, people trusting in the promises of God as we await God's future, as we suffer with each other now. The youth leader's job, then, is to remind adolescents that the resurrection is God's promise to them. It's to remind them that in being near to them, we together can hope in God's future in their most mundane or tragic moments of hopelessness in this world.

BUT WAIT

Okay, you might be thinking, *this all sounds good, but how to I do this? I understand sharing teenagers' place in their suffering though relationships, but how do I proclaim hope in the midst of mundane or tragic adolescent sufferings?*

The truth is that proclaiming the hope of the gospel to youth has more to do with *being* than *doing*. The very presence of your person (your relationship) in their lives is the manifestation of hope. Or to say it another way, the context of your relationship with them not only becomes the way to share in adolescents' suffering, but also by truly being with and for them in their suffering, your relationship is the proclamation of hope. This means you proclaim the future of the resurrection by simply being with them; your person with them becomes the manifestation (the bright picture) of hope. Your person is the proclamation of God's future. If you can live honestly as a human being with them, you *already are* what's needed to be a place-sharer.

Place-sharing, suffering with and for others, is a future reality—a sign of God's future. It reveals a glimpse of the world that awaits us, where we will *fully* be with God. Therefore, in your simple-but-profound willingness to be a place-sharer, you encompass hope within your person! The very fact that an adult would choose to love an adolescent—and love with no agenda but simply the desire to be with them—is an absurd act that bears witness to the future of God. I know that whenever another person has chosen to know me and be with me for only my sake, I have tasted the future; I have tasted the reality of resurrection.

LITTLE MISS SUNSHINE

Dwayne is an eccentric teenager in the movie *Little Miss Sunshine*. He has refused to speak (at all) for a number of months, scribbling any needed communication on a small notepad. His vow of silence was initiated by his distain for his functional but odd family. He decided to stay quiet until he could leave them and begin his pursuit of fighter pilot-dom. The thought of flying jets is Dwayne's greatest hope and the only thing that seems to give him any purpose.

The whole family—including Uncle Frank, who just recently began living with them after attempting suicide—is traveling in a old VW van to Los Angeles for a child's beauty contest in which his beautifully warm, but not-so-pageant-like sister, Olive, is participating. As they race to L.A., Olive passes the time by quizzing Dwayne with eye examination tests she has taken from the doctor's office. Asking him to read each line, he silently gestures his answers. Seeming to have no problems with the smallest of lines, Olive takes out another test, stating, "Now, I am going to see if you're colorblind." Asking Dwayne to tell her what letter he sees inside the reddish circle, Dwayne shakes his head, communicating that he doesn't understand her question because there is no letter. "No, no," Olive counters Dwayne's silent response, "*inside* the circle." Dwayne crosses his arms and shakes his head, indicating he won't be tricked by Olive's little game. "No. See? It's an *A*. Can't you see it?" Olive asks in all seriousness. Dwayne grabs the paper and stares at it intensely; Uncle Frank turns around, stating, "Can't you see it? It's bright green." Dwayne can only shake his head. Turning the other way, Frank utters, "Man!" Sensing something is wrong, Dwayne grabs his notepad to ask Frank what this means. Reading his question, Frank says, "Dwayne, I think you might be colorblind; you can't fly jets if you're colorblind."

The very hope keeping Dwayne alive has withered before him in the back of a VW van. Overwhelmed by disappointment, Dwayne begins to grunt and kick, forcing Frank to demand that

Dad and Mom pull over the van. When they do, Dwayne busts through the doors, racing down a hill and into an empty field, screaming as he runs. Dwayne falls on his knees, planting himself in the field. After getting the story from Frank, Mom makes her way down to Dwayne.

Standing behind him, glancing back over her shoulder, and knowing they are getting dangerously close to being late for the pageant, Mom says, "Honey, I'm sorry. But we need to go. Come on, Dwayne." But Dwayne has no patience for her words that seek to influence him. "I'm not going," he responds. He's suffering the loss of hope and feeling the void of emptiness. But Mom has an agenda, not a malicious one, but an agenda nevertheless. "Dwayne, come on."

"I don't care, I am not getting back on that bus," asserts Dwayne.

"Dwayne, for better or worse we're your family," Mom states. Now Dwayne explodes, having not said anything in months: "No, you're not! I don't want to be your family! I hate you... people! I hate you!" he shouts louder, pointing atop the hill toward the others standing and watching. He continues, "Divorce, bankruptcy, suicide; you're...losers!" Turning back to his mom, Dwayne states, "Please, just leave me here."

Retuning to the others, Mom is baffled; they have somewhere to be, but it's clear that Dwayne isn't cooperating. Finally, they ask sweet Olive to go and talk with him. Gingerly half-stepping down the rocky hill in her cowboy boots, round belly leading the way, she gets to Dwayne, who's sitting on the ground. Instead of standing behind him, pleading with him to get in the van, Olive walks slowly up to Dwayne. Kneeling, she places her arm around him and rests her head on his shoulder, looking out at the desert landscape that now seems so fittingly to represent Dwayne's hopeless future. She makes no pleas, no promises of things getting better or of other fish to fry. No, instead Olive just shares Dwayne's place; she joins his hopelessness by sharing his place.

Then an odd thing happens—an odd thing that connects our understanding of place-sharing with the resurrection. After a while Dwayne stands, helping Olive up from her crouch and then back up the rocky hill. Approaching the others, Dwayne speaks first, "I'm sorry for what I said; I didn't mean it." They give an understanding nod, and back in the VW bus they go. What is interesting for our purposes—and what I think this scene illustrates so powerfully—is how Olive sharing Dwayne's place was not only about joining another in his suffering but also about what happened next. After Olive shared Dwayne's place, he found the strength to hope again, to stand and face the world. Olive's action of place-sharing leads to reconciliation, to a witness of God's future. Returning to the others now that Olive has shared his place, Dwayne asks for forgiveness and receives it, being invited back into the community of the family. His hopes of flying jets have been crashed into a billion pieces, and this dream can never be put back together again. But now standing with Olive beside him, their relationship, her willingness to suffer with him, becomes a true manifestation of hope. Her willingness to stare down his hopelessness, asserting in her presence that he is not alone, is the very tangible power of the resurrection that assures Dwayne that he can stand and hope again—and not only hope again but forgive those who have hurt him. Walking up the hill, Olive having shared his place, Dwayne leaves behind his tactic of silence and is now not only willing to speak but to forgive and be forgiven. This is a taste of the *not yet*. This is a glimpse of the fullness of resurrection.

DISCUSSION QUESTIONS

Why is it important for us to understand Jesus' resurrection as "now" for Jesus but "not yet" for us? (pp. 93-100)

Share about a time in your life when you hoped in God's promises as described on p. 100, even in the midst of death, loss, or tragedy.

Describe someone you know who's a disciple of Christ, as described on p. 100.

On p. 101, Root writes, "The truth is that proclaiming the hope of the gospel to young people has more to do with being than doing." How does Olive demonstrate this in the movie Little Miss Sunshine?

"If you can live honestly as a human being with them, you already are what you need to be a place-sharer." Do you believe this is true?

Into Your World:
The lyrics of the well-known spiritual, "Swing Low, Sweet Chariot," speak of how the hope of resurrection affects daily living: *If you get there before I do...Tell all my friends I'm coming too...I'm sometimes up, I'm sometimes down...But still my soul feels heavenly bound.* Collect a set of songs or poems that express hope in times of pain.

CHAPTER 7

PLACE-SHARING AS GOD'S PRESENCE

It was about 5:30 a.m. I was sleeping deeply and restfully when I was shaken awake by the piped-in pleadings of my son screaming at me through his monitor, "Daddy, Daddy, come and get me, I'm ready to get up!" The problem? I wasn't ready to get up. It was 5:30 in the morning; his (and therefore our) wake up time is usually not until 6:30. I stumbled out of bed and walked to his room, my stiff body reminding me another hour of sleep would be very nice. As I opened his door, the dawn light of an early summer morning hit me as it engulfed him. I should have been moved by the beauty of my two-year-old sitting in his bed, being washed with the early morning sunrise as he awoke to a new day of life. But seeing him sitting in his bed covered with a sunbeam, all I could think was, *Great. I guess there's no way to convince him it's still the middle of the night.* Still feeling unable to function and my body yearning to lie down and rest my eyes, I decided that instead of lying to him (which I wasn't above, it was just obvious it wouldn't work), I decided to bargain with him. So I made my pitch: "Hey Owen, it's still very early in the morning. How about Daddy lies with you in your bed and we listen to a CD and then get up?" To my surprise, he fell for it. So I walked over to his CD player and put in a nice, quiet children's CD, figuring the one called *Sleepy Time Tunes* would be perfect, and crawled into his bed. I shut my eyes to doze off as he laid next to me, chatting away to his stuffed animals and then directing questions toward me just as I would fall deeply into sleep.

About halfway through the CD, a very catchy yet soothing song came on called, "God Is Watching." It went something like...

> Where is God?
> God is watching, God is watching you tonight
> Where is love?
> Love is holding, love is holding you tonight
> And Angels hover over you,
> And Jesus loves you as you are...

Being a theologian, my once sleepy mind—that just minutes earlier sought to lie or bargain with a two-year-old for an hour more of sleep—awoke. Lying on a large teddy bear and surrounded by a stuffed rabbit, three dogs, and a plastic gorilla, my mind started to theologically examine this beautifully soothing song.

I was first struck by the question, *Where is God?* This question really is the heart of the connection between theology and ministry. *Where do we understand God as present? Where is God in the world? How can we help the adolescents we work with encounter this God where this God is? And how can we construct our ministries and times with adolescents to be faithful to where God is?* The singer's question, spilling gently from the rhythm of her acoustic guitar, encompassed a central theological question since the arrival of modernity: *Where is God?* In a world where miracles happen only on TV, death happens in hospitals, and churches sponsor espresso kiosks and Pilates classes, where is God concretely? Where can we say we encounter God?

As much as I admired the songwriter's questions, I was unconvinced by her answer—that God is watching. I found myself unsatisfied. *God is watching* doesn't give me any answers to her question, *Where is God?* (I know, I know, I'm a high-strung theologian, and I should cut her some slack. The song, after all, is not her dissertation, though truth be told it may impact the thinking of the church more than 100 dissertations, so I'll continue.) The songwriter's direct question about where God is concretely, where we encounter God, was answered with obscurity and abstraction. God is watching "somewhere," it seemed; far enough away that God can see us but cannot encounter us. But the question, *Where is God?* asks for a direct, concrete answer. The question assumes a desire to be encountered by God, and encounter is the heart of relationship.[21]

For instance, if my son came up to me while I was watching a baseball game on the couch and asked me, "*Where is Momma?*" and I said "Momma is watching," he would be very unsatisfied; he'd figure I was either a jerk or deranged. He wants to know concretely where she is, so he can be with her, so he can be loved by her and love her. *Where is Momma?*—just like *Where is God?*—is a question that seeks the presence of a person, to be in a relationship with another. To answer, "God is watching," is to assume we cannot share in God's presence, that God is too far away to be with us, to abstract to be a person.

But then what really got me going was the second stanza. "Where is love? Love is holding you tonight." What bothered me wasn't that she equates love with holding and rocking her child (this no doubt is one of the purest acts of love we know). What was disturbing in light of the first stanza was there is no connection between where God is and where love is. (Again, I know this is a children's song and not a theological paper, but this divide between God's presence and our experiences of day-to-day love and care are too often unrelated or unsophisticatedly thought through.) The songwriter had somehow made love concrete: "Love is holding you tonight." She had made it an encounter, a relational reality; but she had made God's presence abstract, that God is invisibly watching you from somewhere unknown.

What our narrative of incarnation, crucifixion, and resurrection points to is neither a God who's far away just watching nor a God who can be divided from the love and embrace of a mother and child. Rather, the narrative of incarnation, crucifixion, and resurrection reveals a God of encounter, a God who desires more than just to watch us but to share our place in relationship, to love us by being present to us. But if this God loves us by sharing our place, how should we understand our encounter with God and how should it impact our ministries?

In my study of relational youth ministries, I have talked with a lot of youth workers about their theological understanding of this ministry practice.[22] When I directly ask them about the theological justification for doing relational/incarnational ministry, they almost always say something like, "Well, because that's what Jesus did; Jesus hung out with a few people, building relationships with them, so that is what we're about in this ministry." What's most interesting to me is that when answering this question, they almost always frame their answers in the past tense: "That's what Jesus *did*." And of course it is what Jesus *did*. But unfortunately, most of the people I talk with usually stop here, which ultimately makes Jesus' life into solely an example. He is more than an example or idea from the past; he's a living person who encounters us still today.

Whenever I walk into a church library, whether it's a conservative or a liberal church, it doesn't take me long to spot Dietrich Bonhoeffer's *The Cost of Discipleship* on the shelf. It seems everyone loves that book. But I often wonder if anyone has really read it. Usually I pick it up and inspect its binding to see if there is any proof that might give evidence that it's been read. Because within this classic Christian text are a number of radical theological assertions. One of them is this: Bonhoeffer asserts, early in the book, that in the same immediacy (in the same directness) that the first-century disciples (Peter, James, and John) encounter Jesus, so we encounter Jesus today. What Bonhoeffer states is that when talking about Jesus Christ, we cannot talk (solely) in the past tense, as though Jesus were only an example or an idea. Rather, Jesus is a living person now moving in the world, calling us to himself, calling us into relationship, just as he did with the first-century disciples. For Bonhoeffer, Jesus Christ, and therefore God, is not locked in the past but is present among us now.

If this is true, if this is what we confess, then the theological reason for relational youth ministry is not simply the fact that, "It's what Jesus *did*." Rather our reasons for relational ministry should have something to do with *where God is*. Or to say it another way, relational youth ministry isn't about getting kids to accept a message from long ago but is rather about participating in the living presence of God together with them, right now.

A relational youth ministry of place-sharing argues that our relationships—where we truly see other persons and share their place—are the location of God's presence in the world. So...if asked, "Where is God?" we would answer that God is found in our relationships. Because God has become human, gone to the cross suffering our estrangement (our *hoatis*), and overcome it with resurrection. Jesus Christ stands with us and for us and beside us. So when we search for God, we don't look outside our world, for God in Jesus has already entered our world. Rather, we search and find God by turning to our brothers and sisters and confessing that God in Jesus Christ stands with/next to them.

This is why in Matthew 25:35 Jesus equates his presence (his "where") with feeding the hungry, clothing the naked, and visiting the prisoner. Since Jesus stands with and for them, that means that what we do "unto" them, as Jesus says, we do unto him. When we enter into relationships of place-sharing, God is concretely present—not just as an idea, not just as a nice thing to say or believe, but as an actuality. Since Jesus Christ is really there, quite literally, what we do to another we do to Christ. For through incarnation, crucifixion, and resurrection, Jesus stands with and for others.

What does this all mean? Primarily that our relationships with teenagers are not tools for influence but rather something more beautiful and significant. Our relationships with youth (and our relationships in general) are the location of God's presence in the world. When we open our lives to teenagers, and they open theirs to us, we're not just doing good ministry. Rather, we are doing good ministry because we're both (kid and adult) communing with God. As we share each other's place, through the power of God's own action in incarnation, crucifixion, and resurrection, we're participating in God's own person.

This is both scary and freeing. At first it may feel very scary to imagine that in your relationship with a pimply faced eighth-grader you're together engaged in the mystery of God in the presence of Jesus. "I though I was just helping with homework or helping out with the youth group," might be your response. But this should be freeing before it's paralyzing or scary. When we believe that relational ministry is about influence, our relationships then are about getting kids to do things and be things, and so it becomes our *job* to get them to do and be these things. When it comes to them taking their faith seriously, it becomes our task to move them in this direction. In this perspective, if you're a confirmation mentor, it becomes your job (yours!) to get them to see the importance of the faith and confirm it. I don't know about you, but I find myself completely inadequate to convince others through my relationship with them that they should take their faith seriously or believe something. I deeply desire this for them, but feel inadequate in my *own* power to make it happen. Many of us, as adults, are still journeying in our faith. But when we assert that God is present in Jesus Christ in relationship (not in where we take the relationship), we are free, because God's presence is not dependent upon us—it's already a reality. Our call is simply to be with youth, to share their place, to see them as they are as we invite them to see us as we are, and in so doing confess that Jesus is present between and with us. We don't have to *do* or *be* anything other than our authentic human selves.[23]

But how do we do this? What might this look like? These are the questions we will take up in chapter eight.

DISCUSSION QUESTIONS

What songs or images of God do you remember from your childhood? Where is God in those songs or images? Nearby? Distant and watching?

Share about a time when you've experienced God's presence among us today.

On p. 111, Root writes, "Our relationships with young people (and just simply our relationships) are the location of God's presence in the world." In what ways is this frightening or freeing to you?

Relationships are often complicated or even painful. Are there relationships in which God is not present?

Into Your World:
Go back and reread some of your favorite Bible verses and stories. Which ones best illustrate God's presence in the world? How do you read them differently when you think about God not being "locked in the past" but "present among us today," sharing our place?

CHAPTER 8

THE SHAPE OF FAITHFUL PLACE-SHARING

I was leaning against his kitchen counter, sipping a freshly poured soda still cracking the ice in my cup. I hadn't known my new ministry partner for long (or been in ministry for long myself) when in the middle of our awkward small talk, the doorbell rang. It was 6 p.m., and I was the invited guest for dinner at his home. He went to the door then left the house and closed the front door behind him while his wife prepared the dinner and hurried the kids to the table, rushing from the microwave to the oven as she readied our meal and her children's. I just stood there, drink in my hand, waiting for him to return, too young and stupid to ask if she needed me to do anything.

As we sat down for dinner, he still hadn't returned. She finally sat, breathed a deep sigh of exhaustion, and began cutting her youngest child's hot dog as I started with the salad. I felt awkward; I was there for dinner because he and I had just started doing ministry together, and he was nice enough to invite me over. But as I spooned the pasta onto my plate, he was gone, and I was sitting with his wife and kids, feeling more than a little self-conscious. He had answered the door and disappeared. I thought this was odd, but she seemed, though annoyed, to see it as regular behavior. Finally, feeling very uncomfortable as the silence mounted, my mind raced to find something to say but could think of nothing. I inquired about her husband's absence. She responded it must be the guys. "The guys?" I asked, worried he had somehow gotten entangled with the mob or something. "You know the guys from his Bible study. They stop by most nights." This didn't seem right, but I was too young to understand why.

We had finished dinner and the ice cream was being placed on the table when he finally came in. "Everything alright?" I asked, assuming one of them must have been suicidal for him to be gone for the last 45 minutes without as much as a word. "Yeah," he responded with a suspicious look. "Yeah," he continued proudly, "they were just coming back from skating." Pausing, he continued, as if to teach me something I can only assume, "I guess that's relational ministry for you; it doesn't just happen nine to five." As he said this, I looked at his family—wife clearly worn out, kids messy from dinner. He'd left his wife, children, and invited guest during dinner to be relational, to be in ministry. And this wasn't abnormal; they stopped by most nights around dinnertime. He'd given his life to being relational with young people, but his relational behavior seemed, from my perspective, to be hurting his family. He was saying he was being relational, but what does that mean, and what does that look like?

Does it mean always dropping everything to be with kids? I can imagine if our nights are only filled with *Family Guy* reruns and snack foods, we might answer, "yes." But what about when our nights are filled with needed rest, time with friends, stories read to our children, and long talks with our spouses? Then must we be so-called "relational," responding to every phone call and every doorbell ring?

Now you may be wondering, *Doesn't all this talk about entering into adolescents' suffering and sharing their place affirm us taking such a stance, to becoming people who're always on call, always available? Wasn't my coworker being a place-sharer? If not, what then would faithful place-sharing look like?* There are four stances faithful place-sharing will encompass. (Note: These are dispositions, ways of being in the world—not clean-cut programs or strategies.)

1. OPEN AND CLOSED

A relationship can only be a relationship if the people in it are able to be both open and closed with each other. We rightly assume that being in relationship with another person means being open to that person, letting that person in, sharing things with that person as he or she lets us in and shares things with us. We often hear this in the midst of frustration; for instance, when a parent, spouse, or friend says, "I don't know what it is, but he just won't open up to me." Yet we too often make the mistake of assuming the major component to any relationship is the ability to be open. While this is important, it's just as important (though this seems counterintuitive to us), that we can be closed with another. Defining it, Bonhoeffer writes, "Be wary of the person who cannot be with others, but be just as wary of the person that cannot be alone."

My marriage is not *only* dependent on being open with my wife. It surely is; but just as important is my ability to be closed, my ability to be myself, to have a self. It is just as important not to allow her or myself to be sucked into enmeshment where we can no longer determine where she begins and I end, no longer be two individual people. The most tragic of marriages are those in which each person seems almost flat, as if neither has had an original thought, dream, or simply a laugh in years. Rather, the health of our marriage is dependent on my wife being herself and me being myself. It's dependent on us not only being connected but being connected as the two distinct people we are. If we cannot be closed, having our own opinions, thoughts, and needs—if we are not free to say, "I need to be alone"—then we cannot be open with each other. If she cannot be closed with me, I'll never be able to share in her distinct life, for it won't be distinct enough from my own life for me to see it as "other" than me and something that must be cherished and loved.

Now, what does this have to do with relational youth ministry? To enter into another's suffering and share another's place demands that I open myself to this other; but just as importantly, it demands that I be closed. If I cannot be closed enough to know myself and teenagers as different from me, then I cannot truly see them.

My ministry partner in the previous story believed being relational in ministry was about being radically open, willing to let kids in at any time and moment. But in so doing he was open without being closed. He became not a human being with needs, dreams, and other people (such as his wife and children) who made him who he was, but a dispenser who existed only to meet adolescents' needs.[24] His ministry was no longer broken person to broken person, but a ministry to consuming kids with a commodity-giving youth worker. To be a place-sharer we have to be able to say, "No," or, "I'm finished," or, "Please don't stop by at dinnertime," or, "I'm on vacation," or, "Call me when the sun is up."

If our ministries are only about influence, then we have every reason to fear ever saying any of the latter, for any good sales rep is "always open for business." But if we truly believe God is present (i.e., that the "where" of Jesus Christ is located) in relationships, then it's vital that these relationships be human person to human person, that they be open and closed, where each person sees the distinct and beautiful humanity of the other and therefore confesses God in the relationship.

Too often we've told volunteers and youth workers that their relational success is judged on how open they are with kids, but it's just as important they be able to be closed. It's important that they identify with adolescents; but just as important is their ability to be different, to differentiate, to be an adult, and to be an individual person. If my ministry partner had gone to the door that night and said, "Hey, guys! Great to see you. But I'm having dinner with my family right now. Can I catch up with you tomorrow?" he would have not only communicated love and fidelity to his family but also (to the adolescents at the door) that he's a distinct human being with others he loves and who love him, with particular thoughts and dreams, with depth in his person that calls those teenagers into their own depth. *He would have become a person to be in relationship with* as opposed to the super-relational pastor he seemed to want to be. When he spent dinner after dinner outside, away from his family, the teenagers who monopolized his time witnessed not a unique person who calls out for relationship with his own distinct, unique person, but simply a guy who met their needs. They saw someone who could be summarized, not as a multidimensional, mysterious person, but as a youth worker whose job it is to be relational. He became as much of a person as the telemarketer who calls me while I'm in the middle of my favorite TV show (*Lost*). The person on the other line is no doubt a mysterious, wonderful human being, but I never witness this because he has opened himself to me only to get me to do something. I haven't witnessed the wonder of his being in his closedness and otherness, therefore I find it easy to ignore him.

My ministry partner that night was right: Relational ministry is not done from nine to five. Sharing another person's place happens at times and places rarely anticipated, and often it is in the middle of crises that we are called to enter others' lives. But the fact that it's not a nine-to-five job doesn't mean it's not human-izing, that relational ministry isn't practiced from the core our beings, which call us to be with everyone (adolescent or not) as open and closed.

I don't know what genetic or psychological flaw we passed on to our children, but both of them had the hardest time learn-ing to sleep. It's the oddest thing for young parents to learn that infants and toddlers have to be taught to sleep when it seems so innate to us. But it's true we have to be taught to sleep; and for some children this comes naturally—but for my children, it was a battle. After months and months of fighting with our son to sleep and feeling as if we were going to literally die from sleep depri-vation, we tried a new approach. (Caution: I tell this story only to make the point about the importance of the open and closed dynamic of relationships—not as a new sleeping method!)

Having hit desperation we realized that it didn't help to pick up our son and then try to put him back down—rather we needed *him* to put himself back to bed. However, we were against forcing him to cry himself to sleep alone. Holding to a theology where the condition of sin is, in Owen-speak, *hoatis* (being all alone cry-ing and no one coming), we refused to allow him to bear this struggle alone. But it was *his* struggle and not our own (believe me, given the opportunity we had no problem sleeping). So we finally blew up the air mattress, put it on the floor of his room, and took turns sleeping on it. When he would awaken and begin to cry, from the air mattress we would turn toward him and say, "Owen, Daddy (or Mommy) is right here, you're not alone; but it's time to go to bed, and I'm not picking you up. Lie down and go to sleep." After a few nights of terrific and tear-filled rage, it sunk in, and he would lie back down and go to sleep. This is what finally worked for him.

What we did by lying on the air mattress and telling Owen to go back to sleep is to live out the open and closed dynamic of place-sharing relationships. We entered Owen's suffering with him, opened ourselves to share his place; he was not alone. Our presence assured him he was held by more than his grief or fear. But by refusing to get up and appease him, we lived out closedness. We asserted with our actions that his suffering and struggle was *his* and not ours. We were with him in the midst of it, and in a real way suffered it, but we would not, as is so easy to do, confuse his situation and person with our own. We would not over-identify. By just lying there we witnessed to our openness and identification but kept a boundary of differentiation that, in the end, provided him with the strength to trust his own being and fall asleep by himself.

The real art of practicing relational youth ministry, then, is not about dropping everything to be with kids; more profoundly, it's about being open and closed alongside them. As a volunteer or a new youth worker, it's not your job to be radically open with young people; it's your job to be a healthy and whole person who's able to both identify with them and be different from them. When recruiting adults to be in the lives of adolescents, I look for those who can live out of this balance more than *anything* else.

2. BARRIER: JUDGMENT AND CONFRONTATION

In the movie *Good Will Hunting*, Will is a delinquent young adult from South Boston. After getting in a fight with someone in the neighborhood and hitting a cop who was breaking up the fight, Will's sentenced to see a psychiatrist or go to prison.[25] Chasing away his first two psychiatrists—by questioning one's sexuality and the other's vocational methods—Will is close to accomplishing his strategy of avoiding this court-appointed hurdle by scaring off all willing counselors. That is, until he meets his last option, Sean. Sean is dealing with issues of his own. Once a promising MIT grad, he's found himself working in a community college teaching uninterested students. Yet, his issues are not really career related; he's still dealing with the death of his wife, who lost a long, painful battle with cancer.

Will enters Sean's office for their first meeting and puts his strategy into action, looking for a way to push Sean to quit before ever starting with Will. Will begins by insulting the books on Sean's shelf; Sean's not bothered. Trying a new tactic, Will asks Sean how much he can bench. When Sean responds with a weight much higher than Will's max, he looks for another angle. Seeing a painting leaning against Sean's window of a man in a boat Will inquires, "Did you paint this?" "Yeah," Sean responds. Taking a few shots at its quality, Will then tries to interpret it. "You ever hear the saying, 'any port in a storm?'—Well, maybe that means you. Maybe you were in the middle of a storm, a big... storm—the waves were crashing over the bow, the...mast was about to snap, and you were crying for the harbor. So you did what you had to do to get out. Maybe you became a psychologist." Sean's not bothered. "Bingo," Sean says. "Now let me do my job." But Will takes one more shot at finding Sean's weak spot through the painting, "Maybe you married the wrong woman." Sean turns quickly and shoots back, "Watch your mouth." Will smiles; he's found Sean's vulnerability, so he goes for the kill, "That's it, isn't it? You married the wrong woman. She leave you? Was she [seeing] someone else?"

Like he's fired out of a cannon, Sean crosses the room, grabs Will's neck, and pushes him up forcefully against the wall. Sean says through the intensity of clinched teeth, "If you ever disrespect my wife again I will end you." And the scene is over.

Whenever I show that scene to groups of youth workers, I call it a deeply, theologically significant moment—a moment that we can build our ministries around. Of course, I'm not advocating you strangle kids (though you may know a few who make you wish that's exactly what I'm saying). Rather this scene shows the power of another person becoming our barrier, the second of our four dispositions of faithful place-sharing.

Sean's act communicates closedness to Will; it boldly communicates that Sean is a human who's known suffering and pain—and this suffering and pain will have to be respected. It is closed to Will; he has no right to use it for his own purposes. In the forceful act Sean asserts, "No, further! This is me, a human being. You will respect my broken humanity, or there can be no relationship." In shooting across the room and asserting his closedness, something beautiful happens, as you'll remember if you've seen the movie. Through this act of closedness, in which Sean becomes Will's barrier, a relationship is formed—and such a rich relationship that Will (and Sean, for that matter) discovers who he is and what he can offer the world because of it.

The power of faithful place-sharing that's both open and closed manifests itself when the other person becomes our barrier or limit. When we come up against their person, we discover who we are. Whenever we're forced to see the other person (and are not allowed to use them, but to really see them), we discover ourselves. It's in interaction with others that we discover our gifts, abilities, and overall uniqueness. We form our very identities as we come up against the barrier of other people. It's only after witnessing Sean's closedness and seeing Sean as his barrier and limit that Will begins, through their relationship, to discover his own person.

The power of relationships in relational ministry is not that they're ideal tools to get kids to do things. Their power is that they offer young people barriers; they offer the other person's humanity as the adolescent's limit. And as such, the relationship becomes the place where adolescents discover their own persons. When we are barriers, when we are our open and closed selves with them, we're able to say powerful things: "You might think you don't have much to offer, but look at how you've helped me." "You may think you have no gifts, but you are so good at..." "You may not know who you are, but I do, you're my friend." "You may think you're unlovable, but look into my eyes, see that I love you."

But to be barriers we need to be ourselves. We need to be open and closed with adolescents; we need to be able to say, "No further; this is me and that is you," just as Sean did with Will (minus the strangling part!).[26] This is the ultimate danger with my ministry partner in the introduction to this chapter. When he became so open to young people that he would skip out of his parenting responsibilities (not to mention his relationship to his wife or obligation to his dinner guest) to be with adolescents, he was forgetting his ability to be a barrier to kids. Instead he became a jungle gym; his relationship with them gave them something to do, but he couldn't claim his otherness enough to become their barrier, to communicate to them who he witnessed them to be.

This being a barrier has another component that must be discussed. It has sometimes been assumed that when doing relational ministry, we should never confront and judge adolescents' negative behaviors or attitudes. The idea is that if we do, we can destroy the relationship and lose the ability to influence young people in the direction we want them to go. So instead we tolerate their negative behaviors and attitudes until we can get them converted and changed.

I suppose it could be misunderstood that a faithful place-sharer will also avoid confronting or judging negative behavior and attitudes. After all, the goal is to be with them, and you may negate the being-with if you are perceived as being judgmental. Now of course, it's true that it's nearly impossible to formulate a relationship through a judgmental stance. I imagine very few relationships in the world start immediately after someone has insulted another person's hairstyle, body odor, spoken perspectives, or thoughts. But, as I have tried to communicate throughout this book, there is mystery in relationship, and one part of this mystery is: Once we have a relationship it is vital; if the relationship is to be real, we judge and confront each other. I say it to my students this way: "You cannot form a relationship through judgment, but once you have a relationship, the relationship is dependent on you confronting and judging each other."

My wife confronts and judges me all the time; it speaks to her love for me. She says things such as, "You know you have a tendency to talk more than listen." "Do you know that when you say that to me, I feel like you don't respect me?" "Be aware that your actions communicate to people that you are unavailable." Such comments of judgment and confrontation deepen our relationship. Although they're hard to hear, her confrontation and judgment are a concrete working out of her being my barrier. She's being the other that I need in order to know myself, and often when our selves are reflected back to us we are confronted with things that need change and work.

As a barrier, the place-sharer in youth ministry is invited to confront and judge teenagers. It becomes part of the place-sharer's job to confront negative and dangerous behavior, not because you're the morality police (this would only destroy the relationship), but rather because as the barrier you must bring to light all those things that may threaten their humanity. There is, of course, a fine line between being a barrier and being a hammer, but the ultimate difference is that a barrier seeks to see the adolescent's authentic humanity as you open up your own to the adolescent. A hammer simply seeks to beat the dents out of a young person without any concern with how or why they're there. But a place-sharer acts as barrier by seeking to understand why the adolescent is entering into risky behavior and then confronting it with your presence, offering the place-sharer's own person as a companion.

FREEDOM WRITERS

The latter is played out in the film, *Freedom Writers*, based on a true story. Hilary Swank plays Erin Gruwell, an educator from a wealthy Orange County, California, community who takes a job teaching English in a difficult inner-city school in Long Beach. Gruwell (known throughout the movie as Mrs. G) has incredible breakthroughs with her students as she invites them to speak and write about their situations and the ever-present suffering in their neighborhoods and families. The class itself becomes a community of shared suffering with Mrs. G as the lead place-sharer.

Toward the end of the movie, one of her students, Andre, has stopped coming to school. Mrs. G is aware that Andre is going through a rough period; his brother has been on trial for a crime he didn't commit and has just been found guilty. She's heard he's begun associating again with local drug dealers. After several days of absence, Andre returns to school. As he walks toward the classroom, Mrs. G, who is welcoming students in, asks Andre to wait for her. When the bell rings, Mrs. G approaches Andre in the empty hallway. She says, looking him in the eyes, "I've heard about your brother's conviction; I'm very sorry." She has just entered into his suffering, naming it, and placing her person within it.

Then she asks, "Is that why you've missed class so much?"

"I had things to do," Andre responds. Mrs. G pauses, tilts her head, and looks at Andre, communicating she knows, communicating she does not approve. She has entered into his suffering, but she has also shown Andre her closedness; she does not agree with his actions in response to his feelings of despair.

"About this," she continues, now holding up a folder. "The evaluation assignment was to grade yourself on the work you're doing, and you gave yourself an 'F.' What is that all about?"

"I feel like that's what I deserve, is all." Andre responds. "Oh, really?" Mrs. G shoots back. "Do you know what this is?" she continues holding up the folder. "This is [an "F you"] to me and everyone in this class. I don't want excuses." Her confrontation and judgment is thick, but she is not simply seeking to beat him down but share his place, to affirm his humanity.

She continues, "I know what you're up against; we're all up against something, so you'd better make up your mind, because until you have the [guts] to look me straight in the eye and tell me this is all you deserve, I am not letting you fail. Even if that means coming to your house every night until you finish the work."

And then she does it. She speaks the powerful words of being a barrier, words that are transformative, to Andre. Mrs. G says, "I see who you are. Do you understand me?" Placing her own person close to his, becoming his barrier, the other who sees him, she continues intensely, "I can see you, and you are not failing."

Mrs. G becomes Andre's barrier; through person-to-person confrontation she has shared his place. All this hard inner-city kid can do is wipe away his tears, for another has loved him enough to be his barrier, to confront his brokenness by sharing in it through her own distinct open and closed person.

3. CORRESPONDING TO REALITY

Faithful place-sharing has a third disposition, a third way of living and acting with youth. This third disposition is corresponding to reality—and it actually has two prongs to it: In its first instance, the place-sharer seeks to *see the world from teenagers' locations*. This does not, as I have just articulated, exclude confronting and making judgments about adolescent behavior and attitudes; but it means we also seek to see the world from their perspectives. We can't be place-sharers if we refuse to allow young people to inform us, whether through conversation or observation, of their world.

Place-sharing is not about getting young people to conform to our world (be it a world of adult perspectives or religious commitments), but to understand their world and how it's impacting their person. In chapter four we discussed the movie *About a Boy* and the scene in which Marcus reveals the anxiety he has that his mom may again try to commit suicide, and Will responds, "F--king eh." In this scene Will is corresponding to reality; he has taken the time to see Marcus' suffering and can only respond from the core of his own being. He has seen the world from Marcus' place, and as the scene ends, Marcus responds that he feels understood, and Will has entered into this difficult situation with him.

Much like Will in *About a Boy*, corresponding to reality with teenagers often happens as we simply spend time with them. Will didn't do anything magical or professional; he simply weekly (or daily) watched the game show *Count Down* with Marcus, and as he did, Marcus revealed windows into his reality. If we can simply spend time with adolescents with the simple-but-profound desire to know them and their realities, we have become their place-sharers.

The second instance (i.e., prong) of corresponding to reality is *confessing Jesus Christ*. Because Jesus is the incarnate, crucified, and resurrected, Jesus has in some way touched everything in the world. Therefore, as we seek to understand teenagers' realities from their perspectives, we can witness to Jesus Christ. This may happen with direct words in which we remind adolescents of Jesus' love for them in the midst of their pain, pointing them to the fact the God made known in Jesus suffers with them. Or it may be over interesting debate as friends have coffee, in which we reiterate the meaning we find in the gospel. There will no doubt be times to speak of the importance of gospel message. But we must not overlook that in our very action, in our very willingness to be their place-sharer, even without direct words, we are witnessing to the power of God's love for them in Jesus Christ; we are witnessing to the gospel.

Many volunteers feel intimidated about sharing the faith story with youth; some assume because of their fear they must not be called to ministry with adolescents. But I want to remind us that the gospel itself is borne in persons, in the person of Jesus Christ and in person-to-person relationships. By your willingness to be with adolescents and to share their place, you are—in your very being and acting—witnessing to the incarnate, crucified, and resurrected God who shares their place in Jesus Christ. There will be moments to speak of the hope we have and the One who calls us to suffer their realities, but the call is first to join God in sharing their place.

4. FREEDOM IN MUTUALITY

There is no "ought" in place-sharing; there is no need to feel guilty that you should be doing this or that with adolescents. There's only the invitation to be human alongside them, to be yourself, and to experience their lives as they experience yours. (This is the fourth and final disposition of place-sharing.) In your relationship with teenagers, you are free—free to share adolescents' place as it works for you and for them. As long as it's mutually humanizing, it need not conform to some master plan. Helping a kid change his oil, making French flash cards, decorating your daughter's birthday cake, or simply sitting together in silence can all be the needed free space for place-sharing to occur. You're free—free to be you with and alongside them.

However, the real power of place-sharing is not in filling these free spaces with tactics to get kids to talk to us, sharing their deepest and darkest fears and worries. Too often we imagine that a good relational youth worker is able to get adolescents to open up and talk, so we carpet bomb them with questions: "How is school? Who are you dating? How is volleyball? How is your prayer life? How are things at home?" and on and on. As any parent or youth worker knows, getting a 15-year-old guy to answer any of these questions with more than two words is a miracle. Rather, in the freedom of this free space, the goal isn't to get them to talk as much is it to allow them to join in our lives, to come close to us and watch as we seek to live faithfully as authentic human beings. The goal isn't to get them to open up to us as much as it is, in silent assertion through our relationships with them, to invite them to come close us, to see us, to be with us, and to watch as we seek to live out this thing called discipleship in fear, hope, doubt, and joy.

Remember: *You already are* what you need to be to be a place-sharer. Now go and be human with kids; ask them to share your place as they share yours; and know that in so doing Jesus Christ is present. You are together sharing in Jesus' person and witnessing to God's future community.

DISCUSSION QUESTIONS

Offer an example of a relationship—in a movie or in real life—in which the people in the relationship "are so enmeshed that each person seems almost flat."

Share about a time when you've been too open with someone. When have you been too closed?

How does being both open and closed to another person enhance the relationship and confess God in the relationship? Share about a time when this was true in your life.

How is being a barrier to another person (through judgment and confrontation) necessary to having a strong relationship with that person?

What's the difference between being a "barrier" to a young person and being a "hammer"?

What does Root mean when he writes (on p. 129), "There is no 'ought' in place-sharing"?

Into Your World:
Consider a relationship in your life. In what ways is it open and closed? In what ways would the relationship benefit from being more open or more closed? How might you make the change?

CHAPTER 9

THOUGHTS ABOUT WHAT PLACE-SHARING MIGHT LOOK LIKE IN YOUR MINISTRY CONTEXT

I was a fly on the wall (that was actually my responsibility). I'd been asked to visit a junior high ministry's Wednesday-night program and observe it, later telling the leadership what I saw and what I thought. A number of things happened that opened up further conversation, but both the conversations and incidents have since disappeared from my memory. As the program began there was nothing unusual; it was a classic, out-of-control junior high night. Kids were running around the room, boys in the back, literally bouncing off the walls as they tried to use their best extreme sports moves to climb them and then freestyle off one wall to the other. The girls whispered and laughed as the leaders worked vigorously to get the kids to sing and play a few games, but they were too busy flirting, hitting each other, or just talking to take direction. There were a few less-than-funny skits and a hastily planned talk. I wouldn't say it was a disaster— just a regular, tiring, junior high night like we've all lived through.

But one thing sticks with me from that night. Toward the end of the evening, the leader took the microphone they'd been using—to no avail—to speak over the kids and said quietly into it, "Okay, everybody, you know what time it is; it's time for us to pray together. We're going to do it like we always do: Someone tells us their prayer request and then someone else volunteers to pray for him or her." As she said this the chaos subsided, a scene I can only imagine to be reminiscent of when Jesus calmed the storm on the Sea of Galilee, leaving the disciples wet, worn, and holding bailing pails or torn sails now on a perfectly calm lake. Talkative girls and hyper boys, who just minutes earlier were seeing how close they could get to kicking each other in the face as they jumped from their chairs, were now still, looking forward, quiet and attentive. One by one about half a dozen kids raised their hands and spoke of deeply raw issues for which they needed prayer. One girl said, "I just need prayer; I'm struggling with it again, and I'm scared, so I need prayer." A boy said, "My mom's cancer is back, so...I need prayer." And other deep suffering sprang forward, and as it did, with the greatest of sensitivity—sensitivity often not credited to junior high students—they prayed for each other. They shared each other's place and bore each other's suffering. And when they finished...they went back to trying to see if they could kick each other in the head and reading gossip-filled notes from school.

This church had asked me to help them become more successful, to somehow use my knowledge of other ministries and research to help them become more dynamic. The congregation's leadership wanted new models and programs and new ways to make their ministry grow in numbers and relevance. They had in their minds the youth ministry "down the street," or the ones they'd grown up in, and felt that this church was missing something. As they pushed in this direction, all I could think about was that moment when the junior high space had become a sanctuary, where the sufferers dressed in Nikes, board shorts, and midriff-revealing shirts had taken their needs and laid them before one another and God. There in that nondescript room that lacked flat-screen TVs, video projectors, and a platform stage that the leadership seemed to covet as marks of success and relevance, adults were sprinkled throughout, sitting with kids, touching and smiling at those who spoke, nodding with them as they expressed their fears and brokenness into the life of the community.

I wish I could say this was the only church that's asked me to tell them how to be more successful, but of course it isn't. With this last chapter I'd like to direct our attention away from such pursuits and instead ask, *What might we specifically do to form our ministries around a relational youth ministry of place-sharing?* This conversation may be grating for those of you seeking to grow the biggest and most notorious ministry in town, but ultimately my desire is to present some ideas (I have no new model or program) of how we might live out a ministry of place-sharing, some ideas that you might take and begin thinking about alongside your ministry.

BEING BEFORE DOING/DOING AS BOUND IN OUR BEING

"Joe is getting better but still does not seem to be really leading this ministry." "Jack just doesn't get it." "To be honest, I'm really mad; my daughter hates going to youth group. She calls it boring and wants more activities." "I remember when I was in youth group we did so many fun things together; I loved it, and I'm sad that my kids aren't getting that." The latter are just a few of the many heated comments I've heard when doing adult educational hours on youth ministry at churches or in consultation sessions with parents and youth ministry teams. Too often it feels like parents and congregational leadership judge successful youth ministries by the number of kids and how much those legions of adolescents enjoy (are having fun in) those youth groups and their activities.

When discussing a relational youth ministry of place-sharing with youth workers, their most common question is, "What if my senior pastor or key parent wants something else?" My response is always the same. First, it's very difficult to change a congregational system, especially when you're not the one with power. For instance, if your senior pastor wants the youth ministry to look one way, and you want it to look another, it will be very difficult for you to change things when the senior pastor (who possesses the power in most congregations) refuses. Of course, the same is true with vocal parents or congregation members; if they were on your search committee and have accrued esteem within the congregation, it will always be an uphill climb. Bringing change to a system is always hard.

That said, if you're called to move toward a relational ministry of place-sharing and beyond the treadmill of influence, then you'll have to be able to make a theological argument for such a change. This is why we've taken so much time examining place-sharing theologically. Because if place-sharing is only another new strategy for doing youth ministry, another kit you can buy to build your ministry, it will always lose in conversation with entertainment and influence-based perspectives. Entering into adolescents' suffering with no other purpose than to be with them cannot compete as a growth strategy with putting the focus on events, concerts, and T-shirts (not that any of this is intrinsically bad; just that it cannot be the heart of any ministry, though some youth ministries have tried).

If you're going to build support for place-sharing in opposition to influence-based youth ministry, you have to make your argument theologically. If it's about what will be perceived as more numerically or monetarily successful, then influence will always win. But if it's about faithfulness to the God of the Cross who meets us in the broken—and then resurrected—humanity of Jesus Christ, then the conversation has changed.

Allow me to contrast these more directly as they relate to our actual *doing* in youth ministry. If your ministry is ultimately about personal influence, getting adolescents to know, commit, and do things, then your ministry is ultimately focused on *how* questions—e.g., *How can we get kids to come? How can get them committed to the group or faith? How can we do the most cutting edge ministry? How can we be successful? How can I do a good job and be esteemed?* But when we do our ministries as place-sharing, we're drawn away from constructing our ministries around the exhausting how and can instead minister from *who* questions: *Who are these young people and what is impacting them? Who am I alongside them? Who are we as a youth ministry team and congregation? Who is this God we serve, and who is God calling us to be and be with?*

If you do ministry in the *how* of personal influence, at the end of the day you're ultimately a programmer. Your job is to construct events and outings that can draw adolescents and keep them coming back for more. Whether you're a paid, professional youth worker or volunteer in the *how* of personal influence, your job is to satisfy kids' entertainment desires so you ultimately gain more opportunities to influence them. It is true that you may also need to share the gospel by leading a Bible study or giving a talk, but this can only happen if you create programs, events, and experiences that keep them coming back for more—even if that's simply through your outgoing, fun, and cool personality that, in itself, becomes a carrot to influence.

What's interesting about this perspective is that it sees adolescents at the level of their (supposed) free will, their ability to choose (e.g., what kinds of jeans to buy or what movies to see) rather than at the deep level of their frail humanity, the level of their brokenness and great joy. We see kids as "deciders" (to borrow a phrase coined by former President George W. Bush), not as human beings seeking relationship in the depth of their humanity. We surely choose our relationships, but for instance, with my wife, it's better to say that in deep relationships we find ourselves choosing rather than that we decide. We find ourselves choosing because in the mystery of our relationships we have tied our beings together and can do no other than choose to spend our lives together.

When we move toward place-sharing, where the focus is on the *who*, we're no longer primarily programmers (though we may still plan events and outings), and instead we become theologians. Because our job is to share adolescents' places, to seek to know their distinct *who* as we confess God's own *who*, we confess that God is actively meeting us through the relationship. Our job isn't to discover the next hot thing or craft our personalities to be hip but to watch for God's activity in our lives and to articulate it. This is being a theologian; it is to be deeply with others as we seek God.

But if we do ministry in the *how* as programmers who see adolescents as ultimate "deciders," we can only in the end evaluate our ministries in light of influence—e.g., *How many? How fun? How many tears? How many conversions? How many attending Christian colleges?* These become the tallies we live by. But if we do our ministries seeking to be near the *who* of adolescents and God, as theologians, the evaluation of our ministries rests in conformity to the narrative of the One who has become incarnate, crucified, and resurrected. Our ministries are successful not when they meet the high tallies in the *how*, but when we are, in humility and weakness, seeking to conform ourselves and our ministries to the *who*—the very narrative that has revealed a God who goes all the way to hell to share our place.

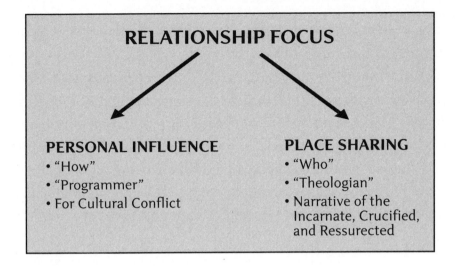

A CONGREGATIONAL PURSUIT

If we're to do our ministries as theologians *who* seek to be faithful to the narrative of the incarnate, crucified, and resurrected God *who* meets us in relationships, then we'll quickly realize that place-sharing is not a job for just youth workers, volunteers, and youth groups. Rather it's a whole congregational pursuit for the sake of their youth in the congregation and community.[27] When parents and congregation members say less-than-upbeat things about their youth workers and youth ministries, they usually speak from the place of the misconception that youth ministry is solely the youth team's job and not their own.

To really get into this discussion of moving the youth ministry into the life of the congregation would take another book, but it must be said if our goal is to really enter the lives of adolescents and share their place; it will take a congregation and its adults to open their own lives and invite young people to join them. This can happen in many different ways; for instance, mission trips not being cohort-based (e.g., the "high school mission trip") but congregation-based, in which all people of all ages are invited and encouraged to serve together. I don't imagine any of this is easy, but it is essential for the future of the church that we think of how we move past the rigid division between young and old in the area of worship and service.

You cannot be in a relationship of place-sharing with every adolescent in your church (unless you only have three or four students). These relationships of shared suffering are too rich and too mutual to allow them to happen with handfuls and handfuls of young people. But each kid does deserve and need someone to share his or her place. Therefore we need the congregation as a whole to open its life and invite young people to be with adults.

PRACTICAL ACTIONS FOR PAID, PROFESSIONAL YOUTH WORKERS

So what are some practical things that paid, professional youth workers can do in moving their ministries toward place-sharing? Let me provide seven that might help you as you head down this road.

• *Recognize there's a difference between connection and relationship.*[28]

As I just noted, it's impossible to be in a relationship of place-sharing with every teenager in your congregation (not to mention those you meet in the community). But there is a difference between a relationship (where we share deeply in each other's person, joining our mutual sufferings and joys) and a connection (knowing a kid's name, grade, school, and perhaps an interest or two). As the paid youth worker, it's your job to have a connection with every adolescent in your youth group, but it is the congregation's job (with you in leadership) to have relationships with all its teenagers. It's important that we don't confuse these. There's nothing wrong or immoral about having only a connection. What's potentially immoral and deeply hurtful is when teenagers believe they're getting a relationship with you, but it's only a connection you've used to influence them toward what you want for them.

Now it is true that parents (and their kids) are going to want you, as the paid youth worker, to be in a relationship with *their* kids and won't be satisfied with a connection. The only way to deal with this, again, is theologically. It is important that you are not only thinking about what your theological conception for ministry is, but also communicating it with the congregation, parents, leaders, and young people. Few of us, for example, believe that it is only those with the title "pastor" or "minister" who are qualified to do ministry; most of us hold to the theological commitment of the priesthood of all believers, that all are ministers of the gospel. It may be true that you are the paid youth workers, but the idea that *only* you are qualified to work with their children is based more on the idea of technical specialties than on theological beliefs. They imagine that because they hire a specialist to fix their computer, since you are trained or paid, you, too, are a specialist; they want the specialist to fix their kid. It is only by giving a new narrative—a theological narrative—that you can change the conversation, moving from the technical realm to the theological.

• *Be a relational matchmaker.*

One of your main jobs is *not* to be in relationships with all the young people in your ministry but to match them up with other adults. Your job as the paid youth worker is to know both kids and adults well enough that you can invite them to share life together. This means you cannot simply go to the *teenager* but must recognize, as the one given the responsibility of advocating for youth, that you must build trust and support with adults as well.

• *Allow for open space.*

This matchmaking can happen in a number of ways, but ultimately what's needed—and we too often forget this—is open space to allow adults and young people to bond. It isn't that place-sharing does away with programs as much as it seeks to provide the open space in such events for adults and kids to meet each other in significant ways. The amount of open space will depend on the group and their ages. Allowing an hour for high school students to hang out, play board games, and just be with each other and adults may work really well. Open space for junior highers may be 15 minutes of an activity that allows adults and kids to share their interests.

• *Recruit and serve volunteer leaders.*

This open space is contingent on adults being present. This means one of the paid, professional youth worker's primary jobs is to recruit and serve volunteer leaders. But recruiting doesn't equate to looking for adults who appear young and cool enough to influence kids; rather it's about inviting adults to be with young people in significant ways. Things will come up, of course, with which adults will need help. There may be family struggles or destructive behavior on the part of adolescents—or maybe just the personal doubts of a leader. The paid youth worker's job is to come alongside and be with the volunteer leaders as they're with kids.

A concrete step you may try in order to move your ministry in the direction of place-sharing is constructing things like retreats and trips in terms of almost 50/50 adults and adolescents. This may seem difficult (i.e., "I have a hard enough time getting one or two people involved, let alone 30!"), but this leads us to our next point.

• *Share the vision.*

Your job is to theologically communicate the vision for place-sharing. You don't have to be the most natural place-sharer (if that's even possible), but it's important that you can communicate both practically and theologically your vision for place sharing. You might do this by preaching, writing newsletters, or providing adult education.

• *Communicate with parents.*

One of the essential groups of people with whom this shared vision must be presented is parents. There's nothing worse than a volunteer going to an adolescent's house to pick him up only to receive suspicious looks or comments from a parent. The job of the paid, professional youth worker is to communicate to parents why other adults may be hanging out with their children and how such interaction is not designed to undermine them but to support the whole family. Most parents would be more than happy to have adults supporting them and their children, but all parents want to understand who these people are and why they're now driving their children across town.

PRACTICAL ACTIONS FOR THE VOLUNTEER YOUTH WORKER

• *Keep it organic and be yourself.*

Please don't have it in your mind that you need to be this or that way to be a youth worker—just be yourself. Allow relationships and the depth of the relationships to happen naturally. The quickest way to destroy any relationship—and maybe you know this from dating experiences—is for one person to demand a level of intimacy or depth to the relationship that the other person isn't ready for or wants. So just be yourself and spend time discussing and doing things that you and the young person enjoy.

• *It's not wrong to spend most of your time with adolescents you enjoy.*

While it's fine to have a few adolescents with whom you spend most of your time—to share their place—beware to not make this an elite or closed group. Continue to work toward connections with other teenagers in your congregation, even if you spend most of your time with a few you enjoy.

• *Include them in your life.*

Give them opportunities to have dinner with your family, to see you in multiple contexts. Of course this must be done keeping the needed open and closed-ness in place, but remember it's through our mutual sharing in each other's lives that we share each other's place.

• *Support their families.*

In spending time with adolescents, view your actions as not only sharing their place but supporting their families. Take time to communicate with parents, sharing your desire to be of assistance in any way, asserting clearly you're present to support them.

• *Pass on the faith through doubt and struggle.*

Don't be afraid to do this. Adolescents don't need adults in their lives who're immune to doubt, failure, and struggle; rather they need adults who can *appropriately* invite them to see and be with them in the midst of such experiences. For instance, rather than viewing confirmation mentoring as helping a teenager understand and commit to faith, you can practice it as the communion of fellow seekers articulating their wonderment and questions about the faith tradition, as they together strive for mutual understanding of each other and the faith tradition.

We've only begun to examine some practical steps as we seek to be place-sharers where God's called us. I now leave it up to you—to flesh out more fully what place-sharing looks like in your context, and more significantly, to share teenagers' places as God in Jesus Christ shares yours.

DISCUSSION QUESTIONS

In what ways are people most pleased (or disappointed) with the youth ministry in your context?

Why is it important to examine place-sharing through a theological lens?

Which "how" questions (p. 138) are most prominent in your context?

What big change in your youth ministry would you most like to see?

Into Your World:
What small step could you take today toward a relational youth ministry of place-sharing?

ENDNOTES

1. A version of this chapter was published in *The Journal of Students Ministries* May/June 2008 in an article titled "The Problem with Relational Ministry."

2. See September/October 2004 *Youthworker* Journal's "Post-Relational Youth Ministry: Beyond youth work as we know it" by Dave Wright and Dixon Kinser.

3. In chapters one and two of *Revisiting Relational Youth Ministry,* I articulate the cultural transitions that brought relational ministry forth. There I show how changes in our culture, youth ministry, and evangelicalism birthed this form of ministry. I argue that Rayburn intuitively understood many of these transitions and was the first to give attention to the high school as *the* location of the American teenager. Following the sociological theory of Anthony Giddens, I discussion how relationships have been cut off from obligation and pre-given structures—such as villages and religious communities—and have become self-chosen. We all, since Rayburn's day, choose the significance or insignificance of our relationships. We are free to find intimacy with whomever we wish. It's against the backdrop of these cultural transitions

that relational ministry is born. To examine this further see chapters one and two of *Revisiting Relational Youth Ministry*.

4. *Young Life* (New York: Harper & Row, Publishers, 1963).

5. *The Youth Builder: Today's Resource for Relational Youth Ministry* (Eugene, Oregon: Harvest House Publishers, 1988), p. 15.

6. *Your First Two Years in Youth Ministry: A Personal and Practical Guide to Starting Right* (Grand Rapids, MI: Zondervan, 2002), p. 84.

7. In *Revisiting Relational Youth Ministry* I pick up on Bonhoeffer's argument that the point of God's action in and through Jesus Christ for us was to make us human as God intended. Bonhoeffer argues that in Jesus Christ humanity is free to be really human before God. The objective of being a Jesus follower, then. isn't about being perfect and having it all together, but being human, being yourself in the light of God's grace in the person of Jesus Christ. See page 90 and following.

8. In chapter three of *Revisiting Relational Youth Ministry*, I take the historical analysis of chapters one and two and look sociologically at relational ministry. I not only interviewed these youth workers, but sought to interpret what I heard through the theory of Christian Smith and Michael Emerson's understanding of what sets the terms of evangelical action. They call this theory the evangelical tool kit and argue that we all live with tool kits we use as we act in the social world. The tools we have and use set the terms for the kinds of action we take. The tools that Smith and Emerson saw at work in conservative Protestants (the creators of relational ministry) were free-will individualism, anti-structur-

alism, and relationalism. The idea was that these tools tend to determine how we act. Therefore, we usually do youth ministry that does not see how large structures (like the economy) impact people and tend rather to see the great way to help people is through using relationships as a strategy (relationalism). This strategic use of relationships (relationalism) has led us, in my view, into the cul-de-sac of influence-based youth ministry.

9. Bonhoeffer, as a Lutheran theologian, sought to articulate a picture of who Jesus Christ is without losing the radicalness of the confession that God became human, that God in Jesus is fully human, fully to the point of taking on death, suffering, and destruction. In *Revisiting Relational Youth Ministry*, I seek to apply this theological perspective of a suffering God found in the full humanity of Jesus Christ seriously for youth ministry. This is the real focus of Part Two of that book.

10. In *Revisiting Relational Youth Ministry* my overall argument is that relational ministry is at a point of crisis; that it has taken too much influence into its bloodstream and needs a theological intervention to keep it from danger. That book seeks to provide that theological intervention. As chapters seven and eight show in that book, relationships are essential to transformation (I provide a model of relational transformation or how and why relationships change us as they do). We can't get rid of relationships because, as *Revisiting Relational Youth Ministry* argues, relationships without influence are what make us human before God and our neighbors.

11. Owen pronounced his word "hoe-tiss."

12. Bonhoeffer in his *Ethics* discusses how a disciple of Jesus Christ must enter into guilt, explaining that if we truly seek to follow Jesus then we must be with people to such an extent that their guilt becomes our own, that their guilt becomes shared. This is a difficult point, but an important one for relational ministry. On page 130 and following of *Revisiting Relational Youth Ministry*, I explore Bonhoeffer's point and what ramifications this might have for relational youth ministry.

13. I explore this concept of place-sharing theologically in chapter six of *Revisiting Relational Youth Ministry*.

14. This is what Bonhoeffer calls "corresponding with reality," something I discuss along with acquiring guilt in chapter six of *Revisiting Relational Youth Ministry*. Will corresponds his humanity with Marcus' reality, with his deep open wound. Will's remarks assure Marcus that he's not alone, that someone else has joined him in his reality.

15. See Bonhoeffer's *Christ the Center* and *Papers and Letters from Prison* as well as *Barth's Church Dogmatics* III.2.

16. Contrasting the *who* and *how* begins the theological reimagination of relational ministry in chapter four of *Revisiting Relational Youth Ministry*. At the beginning of this chapter, I look in-depth at Bonhoeffer's point of the difference between *who* and *how* and then look at how deeply a theological perspective of *how* or *who* changes they way we do ministry.

17. This one line encompasses three broad points from Bonhoeffer in chapter four of *Revisiting Relational Youth Ministry* (see page 88 and following). Unlike many of the youth ministry writ-

ings on the incarnational ministry, I follow Bonhoeffer in emphasizing the humanity of Jesus Christ. Too often we have thought more in categories of Jesus' otherness than in the power of the incarnation to communicate the actuality that God becomes near to us in our humanity, therefore freeing us to be human, freeing us to recognize the nearness of God to our broken humanity.

18. One of the major themes throughout *Revisiting Relational Youth Ministry* is the idea of suffering. Suffering has not been a theme picked up much by youth ministry, but it's central to many of our theological traditions, especially those of us who trace our history back to the Reformation. In *Revisiting Relational Youth Ministry*, I dialogue with Bonhoeffer because of his elegant way of picking up this theme in the context of relationships. The central place of suffering is seen in Luther's theological bracket through what he calls the "theology of the cross," in which Luther chooses to start his understanding of God with God on the cross of suffering.

19. In chapters seven and eight of *Revisiting Relational Youth Ministry*, I sketch out in diagram form what this transformational process through suffering relationship looks like. I use a story about Kelly and Mandi and Sean and Will (from *Good Will Hunting*) to provide narrative to this theory of transformation.

20. This is another important point I've picked up from Bonhoeffer and delve deeper into in Part Two of *Revisiting Relational Youth Ministry*.

21. This idea of asking, "Where is God? Where do we concretely meet God?" was one of the main questions *Bonhoeffer* sought to solve in his own theology. Bonhoeffer was writing in a time

(the end of time) when miracles and easy, pre-given concepts of God could not be leaned upon in answering big questions. You couldn't simply assume God's presence but had to, in a scientific modern world, articulate how a God outside of time and space was present within it. This desire to answer the question, "Where is Jesus Christ?" is very significant for those doing ministry with youth. If we are about more than programs and influence, then we must form our ministries around how we would answer this question, "Where is Jesus Christ?" In chapter five of *Revisiting Relational Youth Ministry*, I explain how relationships, human-to-human relationships, are the places *Where* God is concretely present in Jesus Christ among us today.

22. See www.faithfulpractices.org/9999 for more.

23. In *Revisiting Relational Youth Ministry*, I drive these points deeper, looking at a theology of the church and world, examining how human-to-human relationships (me to you) are the concrete presence of God in Jesus Christ.

24. There's more theoretical depth to this understanding of being open and closed than I have space for here. If you're interested, see page 119 and following of *Revisiting Relational Youth Ministry*. The theme comes up through the final three chapters as well.

25. There's a great deal of relational-theological depth in this movie. I use it to look theologically at relationships in chapter seven and eight of *Revisiting Relational Youth Ministry*.

26. You can find more discussion on being a barrier in part two of *Revisiting Relational Youth Ministry*.

27. In the final chapter of *Revisiting Relational Youth Ministry*, I explore a rethinking of youth ministry, youth pastors, and congregations in light of place-sharing. I examine more in-depth the issue of moving youth ministries into the life of the congregation here.

28. I look at this more in-depth at the end of chapter eight and the beginning of chapter nine in *Revisiting Relational Youth Ministry*.

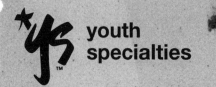